Canadian Rail Travel Guide

By Daryl T. Adair

Dedicated to Gladys Thompson, who impressed upon me my own family's rail history, and nurtured my love for trains and travel at a very young age. Thanks, Grandma!

A **Railfare** *Book*

Fitzhenry & Whiteside

Published in Canada by Fitzhenry & Whiteside
195 Allstate Parkway, Markham, Ontario L3R 4T8

Published in the United States by Fitzhenry & Whiteside,
121 Harvard Avenue, Suite 2, Allston, Massachusetts 02134

www.fitzhenry.ca   *godwit@fitzhenry.ca*

10 9 8 7 6 5 4 3 2 1

National Library of Canada Cataloguing in Publication

Adair, Daryl
        Canadian rail travel guide / Daryl Adair.

Includes index.
ISBN 1-55041-831-9

1. Railroad travel—Canada—Guidebooks. 2. Canada—Description and travel. I. Title.

FC38.A55 2003   917.104'647   C2003-903426-7

U.S. Publisher Cataloging-in-Publication Data
(Library of Congress Standards)

Adair, Daryl.
    Canadian Rail Travel Guide/ Daryl Adair.— 1st ed.
160 p. : col. photos. , maps ; cm.
Includes index.

Summary: Guidebook to rail travel including descriptions of points of interest, locations of
communities along the routes, route histories, overviews of destination attractions, contact
information, etc.

ISBN 1-55041-831-9 (pbk.)

1. Canada — Description and travel — Guidebooks. 2. Railroad travel – Canada —
Guidebooks. 3. Railroad travel — Canada — History. I. Title.
    917.104/ 64 dc22 F1017.A33 2004

Fitzhenry & Whiteside acknowledges with thanks the Canada Council for the Arts, the
Government of Canada through the Book Publishing Industry Development Program
(BPIDP), and the Ontario Arts Council for their support of our publishing program.

All photos by the author unless otherwise credited

All maps by Hilt Friesen.

Cover and page layout design by Hilt Friesen

Printed and bound in Canada by Friesens of Altona

Contents

The Excursions

About the Author

From his youngest days at his family's summer residence, Daryl Adair can remember watching with fascination the passenger and freight trains that passed on the opposite side of Lac Lu, Ontario.

Daryl's grandmother had told him that his great grandfather, who worked for the *Canadian Pacific Railway*, was a member of the CPR committee that chose Lac Lu as a destination for railway workers' families. When she took him on a trip from Vancouver to Winnipeg on *The Canadian*, he became forever hooked on rail travel, and travel in general.

Some years later, he explored Western Canada on his own and subsequently planned and executed a 1997–98 around-the-world journey, travelling by train in England, northern and eastern Europe, as well as on the *Trans-Siberian Express* and railways in China.

His passion for rail travel and touring Canada led him to author *The Guide to Canada's Railway Heritage Museums Excursions and Attractions*. The launch of that book was followed by an extensive period researching the mile-by-mile highlights of all the rail passenger routes in Canada, resulting in the *Canadian Rail Travel Guide*.

Daryl Adair holds a diploma in Tourism. He has contributed articles to the Canadian Tourism Commission publication *Tourism*, to *CN Lines, Branchline, Canadian Rail*, as well as many other publications and websites. He was editor of Winnipeg Railway Museum's heritage newsletter *The Milepost* for five years.

Daryl Adair with *Canadian Pacific Railway* steam locomotive 2816, after travelling past Lac Lu, from Kenora, ON to Winnipeg, MB in the summer of 2003.
Ken Praymak photo

Residing in Winnipeg, Daryl owns and operates Rail Travel Tours, packagers of Canadian rail travel, accommodation, and sightseeing activities. This enables Daryl to share his passion for "riding the rails," and his "insider knowledge" about trains and interesting side-trips, with fellow travellers.

Despite the demanding schedule, Daryl still finds time to volunteer on committees that promote Winnipeg and Manitoba… to cheer out for the Canadian Football League's Winnipeg Blue Bombers football team… to spend time with his nieces and nephew at the Lac Lu family cottage… and to continue exhibiting the same love of travel first experienced in his youth, still watching those fascinating trains go by, way over on the other side of the lake.

Foreword

To travel by train to all of Canada in a single journey, or even in a single season, is no small challenge. It takes the work of many individual efforts to make it all come together. My sincere thanks to all of the people who made the many trips—and therefore this book—possible. My sincerest apologies to anyone who may have been overlooked. I hope each of you gets the chance to dip your feet into the three oceans that surround Canada as I have.

In addition to my family—who helped foster my love of train travel—my thanks are extended to each of the very helpful people whose knowledge, enthusiasm, and support encouraged me to put this book together:

Starting in the East with, Randy Brooks and Kelly Duggan, Nova Scotia Tourism and Culture, Antonella Ferrara, Windsor and Hantsport Railway, Frank Dakai, Vincent Young and Carl Tobin, VIA Halifax. David and Pat Othen. Nancy Wolstenholme, Valerie Kidney and Jeannine Wilmot, New Brunswick Tourism. Isabel Gill and Darlene Anderson, Tourisme Quebec, Béatrice Joseph at Le Québec Maritime, Madame Bedards, Les Motels de la Vielle Gare, Nancy Murray, Chateau Frontenac, Marie-Claude Goyette at Tourism Saguenay-Lac Saint-Jean, Julie Belanger, Holiday Inn Saguenay, Randa Napky, Abitibi Region, Guylaine Larouche and Richard Dumais, the Motel Senabi, Caroline Des Rosiers, Queen Elizabeth Hotel, Tom Little, Manager US Market Development VIA Rail, Francois, Pam, David Gaudette and Len Thibeault for the guided tours of Rue St. Denis, Rey Stephen and Tom Boyd, Tourism Ontario, Deneen Perrin and Jennifer Salo, Chateau Laurier, David Monaghan, Canadian Museum of Science and Technology, Douglas N.W. Smith, James Brown, Joyce Beam, Canadian Ecology Centre, Maureen Reynold, Ontario Northland Railway, James Pereira, Station Inn. Paul Grant, Cochrane Railway Museum, Brian and Ann West, Lois Coo, Peter Browne, York Durham Heritage Railway, Lori Bursey and Ron Keffer, Kolene Elliot and Julie MacNeil, Royal York. Mike Taylor, Fairmont Hotels and Resorts, David Henderson, Railfare, Eric Smith, South Simcoe Railway, Bob and Karen Kertcher, Victor Ferraiuolo, Tourism Niagara, Charles and Anne Becket, Ron Broda, Discovery House Museum,

Troy Rainville, Quality Inn Sudbury, Dale Wilson, Jim Cockburn, Bruce Lafleur, Quality Inn, Michael Morrow and S.K. Hopkins, Algoma Central Railway, Gerard and Marcel Grondin, Companion Hotel. Collette Fontaine, Travel Manitoba, Tom and June Adair, Laura Finlay, Bert Swan, His Worship Michael Spence, Churchill, Bert Couisineau, Paul Legault, Heritage North, Robin Henry, Wescana Inn, Sherraine Christophersen, Fort Garry Hotel, Stafford Swain, CN SIG (CN Special Interest Group), Parallax Information Systems for technical assistance, Morgan Turney for his guidance, Felix Lesiuk, Murray Hammond, Lloyd Smith, Paul Pihichyn, Winnipeg Free Press, Larry Updike, CJOB, Peter Abel, Hilt Friesen for his computer skills, the Winnipeg Railway Museum, Melissa Graham (whose book travels with me), Peter Thiessen, official luggage supplier of UN Luggage, Gary Dy and all the staff at VIA Rail Winnipeg. David Freeman at Tourism Saskatchewan, Jan Desrosiers, Tourism Saskatoon, Cal Sexsmith. Maria Crump and Karen Taylor, Travel Alberta, Jim Lanigan, David J. Walker, Royal Canadian Pacific, Mark Seland, CPR, Edna Holme, Nancy Jackson and Maryse Gallant, Jasper Park Lodge, Kathy Glenn, Jasper Museum, Mike McNaughton, Brenda and Bryanna Bradley. Cindy Burr, Tourism BC, Daryl, Kristine, Grant and Amanda Moulder, Elaine and Lloyd Comish, Kelley Glazer, Ramada Prince George, Sonja Penner, Pacific Inn, Sally Chiang and Robert Hart, BC Rail, Sarah Good, Hotel Vancouver, Janice Greenwood, Rocky Mountaineer, George Devlin, Samantha Gear, Empress Hotel, Don Evans, Bill Johnston, Gordon Hall, Bill Watson, West Coast Railway Association, Joe Volk, Dawson Wolk of VIA Rail Vancouver and a special thank you to Aurelio Macaraeg for his support of the project from the very beginning.

Taking the train to visit any part of Canada is pure enjoyment. The sense of adventure that comes with each mile of steel rail travelled makes each destination, and every journey, unique.

Some of my earliest memories come from spending the summer months, with my grandmother, at our family cabin at Lac Lu, Ontario, watching passing trains on the *Canadian Pacific Railway* mainline. My grandmother told me how my great-grandfather worked for the CPR in Winnipeg, and chose our lake as a summer destination. Another fond memory is of travelling with my grandmother and mother by train from Vancouver to Winnipeg when *VIA Rail Canada* was in its infancy—a trip I will never forget! Who knew where it would lead?

Your Journey Begins

Information and Reservations

You could spend an entire summer travelling in Canada by train, so it will help to do some preparation before you begin your journey. First, research the train timetables for each of the trips you wish to take. These schedules can be secured from the various rail passenger providers at the contacts listed in each "Route Chapter" of this book, or from Canada's national rail passenger provider at the following:

> VIA Rail Canada Inc.,
> 3 Place Ville Marie, Suite 500,
> Montreal, QC H3B 2C9
> 888-842-7245
> *www.viarail.ca*

For a rail travel package you may also contact the author's tour company:

> Rail Travel Tours.
> Box 44, 123 Main St.
> Winnipeg, MB R3C 1A3
> 866-704-3528
> *railtraveltours@mts.net*
> *www.railtraveltours.com*

Timetables commonly describe the types of services available on each route, and provide instructions on booking tickets and other travel information. Many Canadian rail passenger providers make their schedules available on their websites. We have included these at the beginning of each listing. Be sure to confirm the days on which trains operate, as well as connection times and frequencies. Reservations are very important, especially during the peak spring, summer, and fall seasons when some trains may be sold out.

Baggage

Personal baggage restrictions vary by the train route you are travelling. VIA guidelines ask that customers limit themselves to two pieces of carry-on baggage. These should be no larger than 66 cm x 46 cm x 25 cm (26 in. x 18 in. x 9 in.) and weigh no more than 23 kg (50 lb.).

On trains with a baggage car, luggage not needed on the journey can be shipped/stored and picked up upon arrival at your final destination. You will be required to check-in at least one hour before departure at larger stations. Some trains allow you to bring along bicycles, canoes, and, in some cases, even snowmobiles. There will be a surcharge for larger items such as these. Whatever you bring, attach a proper tag with your correct name and address.

Getting to Canada

Numerous airlines fly to Canada from international and overseas locations. Canada's largest airline is Air Canada. Its routes and flights can be researched at *www.aircanada.ca*. Rail routes connecting Canada to the United States also provide a popular way to reach the country. These include: Amtrak's *Adirondack* (Washington DC–New York–Montreal); *The Maple Leaf* (New York–Niagara Falls–Toronto); the Amtrak-VIA joint train, *The International* (Chicago–Sarnia–Toronto); VIA's corridor service from Windsor, located across the river from Detroit; and on the west coast, Amtrak's *Cascade* (Seattle–Vancouver). All trains are subject to customs inspections when crossing the Canada-USA border. To help the border officials, you will be asked your nationality when reserving the ticket.

Currency, Taxes and Gratuities

Canadian currency is based on 100 cents to the dollar. Coins are in denominations of 5¢, 10¢, 25¢, $1.00, and $2.00. Canadians generally refer to their one and two dollar coins as the 'loonie' and 'toonie' respectively. Across the country there is a 7 percent national Goods and Services Tax as well as provincial sales taxes that vary across the country (except in Alberta which has no provincial sales tax.) In the Atlantic Provinces the two sales taxes are "harmonized" into a single tax surcharge. Out-of-country visitors, with your saved receipts, can file a claim to secure a GST rebate. It is quite common to leave gratuities after a meal, or for sleeping car attendants and dining car staff, especially when exceptional service has been provided.

Breaking up Your Journey

This guide lists contact information for Canada's local and regional tourism authorities along the various routes. Suggested accommodations are included at the beginning and end of many "Route Chapters." It is highly recommended that reservations be made well in advance of your planned visit.

How to Use this Guide

The *Canadian Rail Travel Guide* begins with regularly scheduled passenger trains, geographically from east to west. The later portion of the book lists excursion train routes in the same east-to-west manner. The text describes highlights in various directions from the rail line. Finally, the book's clearly marked maps enhance the text and make it convenient to use for travel in either direction.

Railway Subdivisions

To determine where you are, you must first identify the railway subdivision in which you are located. These subdivisions traditionally begin at the eastern point (Mile 0) and accumulate miles travelling to the western end of the subdivision where another will begin. Historically, these divisions were about 125 miles in length, based on the distance between various water and refueling stops that a steam locomotive could travel in a shift. They were named primarily after prominent communities in the area, the region where the subdivisions are located, or even after railway financiers. Because modern diesels travel these lengths much more quickly, with fewer servicing stops than a steam locomotive required, many of these have now been combined to form longer subdivisions up to and exceeding 250 miles. At some places railway subdivisions intersect with other railway subdivisions, not at the beginning of mile 0, therefore mile markers may vary. Refer to the accompanying maps for where your train is located on the subdivision you are travelling on. In some cases, the map will indicate a mileage that differs from a reference in the text, because *stations* are sometimes located a short distance away from the river, lake or community of the same name.

Mileposts/Mileboards

Each mile of a railway subdivision is counted off by a milepost. Look for a small sign, with black lettering on a white background, attached to steel posts or former tele-graph poles. Mileage markers can also be located on bridge ends, signal masts, and the reverse side of road crossing signs.

Station/Siding Names

Names are another easy way to locate where you are. You'll see them featured on the end of the stations. Names of sidings are commonly identified on a white sign with black lettering.

Scheduled Stops

Many scheduled stops provide only a few minutes for passengers to depart or join the train. In larger cities, and at some service stops, you may have a somewhat longer respite, providing the opportunity to stretch your legs alongside the train or visit the station.

Onboard Staff

The structure of the staff varies by train route. The person in charge might be the Conductor, Service Manager, or Train Manager. This individual is responsible for the crew and the safety and smooth running of your journey. Many of the excursions in Canada are operated by volunteers who provide a wealth of information regarding the area's rail history and its other attractions.

Options and Services

Most VIA onboard staff, as well as staff in the larger stations across the country, are able to serve passengers in Canada's two official languages, French and English.

The seating options depend on the particular route. VIA's overnight trains offer a variety of travel options: economy-class seating with large reclining seats, upper and lower sections, roomettes/single rooms, bedrooms/double rooms, and drawing rooms/triple rooms. In the Windsor–Quebec City corridor, you can choose from economy or class coach-style VIA 1 seating. The remainder of the country's trains feature comfortable coaches with large seats. Equipment on excursion trains varies from turn of the century wicker chairs to modern Gold Class dome cars on the *Rocky Mountaineer*.

Food options also vary. A majority of trains offer take-out service from a café car or snack bar. Sometimes, meal service comes in the form of a dining car or a sandwich/snack and beverage cart/counter on your coach. Meal sittings in the dining cars may be very busy, so reservations for lunch and dinner (where available) are recommended.

Freight Trains

Freight trains move many of the goods and products required by consumers in many nations. It will be a common occurrence that you will pass seemingly endless freight trains, carrying everything from Canadian grain, lumber products, coal and ore for export to new vehicles, television sets, and toilet paper for consumers at home. Because of the pulling power of the modern diesel locomotives, the lengths of these trains can often be longer than many of the siding tracks that allow trains to pass each other, which means that the passenger train is the one that must wait in the siding to allow the long freight train to pass by.

Photography

Use at least a 200-speed film to take pictures from a moving train. Whether using a film or digital camera, these same rules apply:
- avoid the reflection inside the car by getting the camera lens as close to the window as possible
- watch the maps and mileage markers for recommended locations
- avoid shooting into the sun
- make sure you have lots of film in your bag

Further Reading

Following are some books to enhance your journey across Canada:

The Guide to Canada's Railway Heritage by Daryl T. Adair. Sister guide to this publication features numerous railway museums, attractions and excursions in each province. North Kildonan Publications, 2001.

Trans-Canada Rail Guide by Melissa Graham. City overviews and highlights of some of Canadian rail routes. Trailblazer Publications, updated 2003.

The Ocean

Shaped by the sea, Halifax—the capital of the Province of Nova Scotia—has a profound history. Named after the second Earl of Halifax, George Montagu Dunk, it was first developed by the British. They founded a base here in 1749 to counter the French fortress to the north in Louisburg. Shortly thereafter, New France was captured and the base became a symbol for British dominance in the North Atlantic. Its strategic importance was enhanced when the colony of New England left British rule.

The city's unique history continued into the 18th century and was linked closely to the events of the sea. Waves of immigrants looking to start a new life had their first contact with the New World in Halifax. In 1912 the city became linked with the sinking of the *Titanic*, 150 of those who perished are buried in Halifax cemeteries. Then, on December 6, 1917, the Norwegian vessel *Imo* collided with the French munitions ship *Mont Blanc* which caught fire, and exploded, wiping out a good portion of North Halifax, and, together with the fire that followed, killed 1,700 and injured over 4,000.

Today, the city continues its close relationship with the sea. Halifax is a very busy commercial seaport, and is the base of operations for the Canadian Navy's Atlantic operations. The city centre is well laid out,

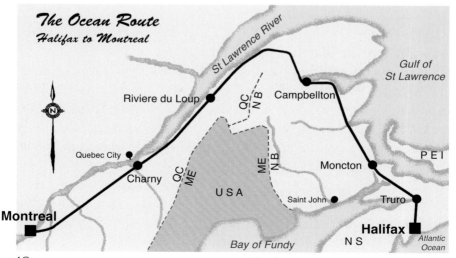

The Ocean Route
Halifax to Montreal

12

with numerous attractions located within walking distance. For your travel base in Halifax, the Lord Nelson Hotel is recommended. It is conveniently located at 1515 South Park Street across from the Halifax Public Gardens and on the corner of Spring Garden Road.

Visitors to the city will enjoy the Halifax Citadel National Historic Site where you can take a guided tour and journey back in time to see the 78th Highland Regiment in action. Another highlight is Pier 21, where many immigrants transferred to the train to take them west. One display features a rail car that takes you on a simulated journey across Canada. The Maritime Museum of the Atlantic, located at 1675 Lower Water St., is a must see, with numerous displays including the *Titanic* exhibit and the impressive Halifax Explosion display. The *HMCS Sackville*, moored behind the site, is open in the summer for visitors.

Before you go, you may wish to contact Nova Scotia Tourism & Culture, PO Box 456, Halifax, NS B3J 2R5.

Phone: 800-565-0000. Web: *www.exploreNS.com*

The Dominion of Canada was formed when the provinces of Ontario, Quebec, New Brunswick, and Nova Scotia joined together on July 1, 1867. At the time, there were three separate railways in the region—the *European & North America Railway*, the *New Brunswick and Canada Railway,* and the *Nova Scotia Railway*. Each line was isolated, but played an interesting role in the early commerce of the regions it served. In fact, the *Nova Scotia Railway* was one of the first to operate an early "piggyback" service, hauling farmer's wagons and stagecoaches on flatcars. To these a fourth railway was added—*The Intercolonial Railway*, which was needed to connect the Maritime Provinces to the rest of Canada.

The first run of *The Ocean Limited* was on July 3, 1904. In 1918, the *Intercolonial Railway* fell under the control of the Canadian Government Railway, which later became the *Canadian National Railways*. Today, operated by VIA with the named changed to simply *The Ocean*, it is the train that has been longest operating in Canada.

Your journey begins next to the Westin Nova Scotian Hotel, at the *VIA Rail Canada* station located at 1161 Hollis Street. Built circa 1929, the exterior features an impressive Greek-Roman style. As you pass the four columns at the entrance, the station opens up to a large concourse, which is well lit with numerous skylights.

Route Highlights

Halifax to Truro
Bedford Subdivision

Miles 0–10: Whether arriving or departing Halifax, look to the south to see the National Historic Site Pier 21, where millions of immigrants entered Canada.

From miles **1** to **3** the route takes you through the city in a unique rock cut, believed to be built after the Halifax explosion to keep the tracks away from the harbour in case a similar incident ever occurred. (The original route was wiped out, along with the *Intercolonial Railway's* Halifax Station.) At mile **4.6**, look north to see the wooded Fairview Cemetery, which has 121 graves from the Titanic tragedy, the largest location of such graves in one cemetery in the provincial capital. The Bedford Basin is visible to the north from miles **5** to **10**. Edward, Duke of Kent (father of Queen Victoria), built the round building to the north at mile **7** in the late 1790s as a music pavilion. Today this unique building, with its white columns and green roof, is a private residence. If you look to the east you can see the A. Murray Mackay Bridge which joins Halifax to Dartmouth. Below the bridge is the Narrows, where the 1917 Halifax Explosion occurred.

Miles **11–64:** As you move away from the city the scenery changes to a forested area with lakes and cottages. The track that turns to the west at mile **15** (Windsor Junction) is the *Windsor and Hantsport Railway*, formerly the *Dominion Atlantic Railway*. The *Evangeline Express* summer excursion train runs north of here along the Minas Basin. Behind the trees to the east, from miles **1** to **20**, sits Lake Kinsec. You cross the Nine Mile River as you pass through the town of Elmsdale at mile **32.4**. This is the site of the first iron railway bridge in North America, built in 1877. At mile **47** watch for salmon fishermen as you pass over the Stewiacke River. When you arrive at the Truro station, located in the Truro Centre Mall (mile **64**), the tracks for the *Cape Breton & Central Nova Scotia Railway* and the continuation of VIA's *Bras D'or* swing to the north.

Moncton 124.9
Calhoun 110.3
Upper Dorchester 100.4
Sackville 86.7
Amherst 76.8
Maccan 68.1
59.6
52.6
48.7
Springhill Jct
Salt Springs
Oxford Jct
Atkinson 37.7
Folly Lake 24.0
Londonderry 17.1
Belmont 7.7
Truro 64.0/0.0
Hyde 61.5
Brookfield
Alton 51.2
Stewiacke 46.7
Shubenacadie 42.2
Milford 38.4
Elmsdale 32.1
Sandy Cove 27.0
Kimsac 20.0
Windsor Jct 15.8
Rockingham 6.0
Halifax 0.0

Atlantic Ocean

14

Route Highlights

Truro to Moncton
Springhill Subdivision

Miles 0–23: The route of *The Ocean* ascends out of Truro for the next few miles. The Debert River (mile **11**) is the start of what was known as the "Grecian Bend," due to the politics that shaped the route the line takes. Apparently the owner of the ironworks on the other side of the Copequid Mountain, James Livesay, had more sway than the railway engineer Sandford Fleming, who preferred a more practical route; Livesay won out and the tracks travel away from the route Fleming suggested. The bridge at mile **14.5** sits 26-metres (85-feet) above Folly Lake, so-named after a settler's wrong decision.

Miles **24–79:** Keep your camera ready between miles **24** and **30** for a break in the trees to the north and some fantastic views over the Wentworth Valley. The route is now high above the Wallace River. Watch for the ski slope at mile **29**. Your camera may again be busy between miles **31** and **33**, this time looking south to the row of forested mountains, with Sugarloaf Mountain in the background. After passing through the picturesque village of Oxford Junction, you cross a 126-metre (415-foot) bridge over the River Philip at mile **47**. Coal mining began in the area around Spring-hill in the 1870s and was the mainstay of the region's economy for many years to follow. Today, the mines no longer produce coal, but many tributes in the area praise the brave men who earned their living underground. At mile **70** the scenery starts to change as the train approaches the Cumberland Basin. The large brick station in

Young ladies dressed in period costumes in front of the statue of 'Evangeline' at Nova Scotia's Grand Pre National Historic Site.

Amherst at mile **76.8** was built in 1903. As you depart Amherst, *The Ocean* travels through the Trantramar marsh, a Canadian Wildlife Service sanctuary that is home to blue-wing teal, Canada geese, black ducks, and marsh hawks.

Miles **80–124:** While crossing the Missaquash River at mile **80.1**, you also cross the provincial border between Nova Scotia and New Brunswick. This land bridge between the two provinces is known as The Isthmus of Chignecto. Watch for Fort Beausejour, a National Historic Site, on top of the hill to the north, between miles **81** and **82**. Built by the French in 1751, the fort fell to the British forces in 1755 after a two-week siege. The British renamed it Fort Cumberland and abandoned it in 1835. It was declared a National Historic Site in 1926. The four gravestones on the side of the hill, close to the track, indicate the location of a nineteenth-century cemetery. In 1998, modern archaeological surveys using a ground-penetrating radar unit identified over 40 burials in this area. At mile **85.6** the train crosses the Trantramar River over a 152-metre (500-foot) long bridge, then stops at a historic stone station in Sackville. Look to the south at mile **90.7** for a glimpse of a World War I tribute, featuring a cannon carved into the boulder close to the tracks and a clearing in the forested area. A local railway worker, who switched over 30 trains a day here during the war, erected this as a memorial to all those who left the area to fight overseas. The ominous building atop the ridge to the north at mile **98** is Dorchester Correctional Facility. In front of this is some unique architecture in the form of row houses (known as Keillor House). At mile **104**, look north to see how a construction company has found a new use for railway boxcars— as storage buildings. The tracks slip past quarries on either side of the route at mile **108**. Get your camera ready to take a picture of your entire train on the curve at mile **109**. As you travel through Moncton, look north at mile **123** to see the circular concrete walls that encompassed the Sunny Brae ice skating rink, which opened in December 1920. On February 15, 1928, while attending an indoor carnival in fancy dress, a young lady came too close to an open gas heater. Her outfit caught on fire; seven days later she died of massive burns. Four days later the roof and interior was gutted by fire. The rink was never rebuilt.

Moncton is known as the heart of the Acadian region, and the Acadian Museum is located on the Moncton University campus. An admission is charged. For information call: 506-858-4088.

If you plan to visit the city of Moncton and its famous Magnetic Hill, or plan to stay in the province for an extended period, we suggest you contact: Tourism New Brunswick, PO Box 12345, Campbellton, NB E3N 3T6, or telephone: 800-561-0123. Web: *www.tourismnbcanada.com*

The Atlantic Ocean seen just beyond a community in New Brunswick.

The Ocean — Contact information on page 7

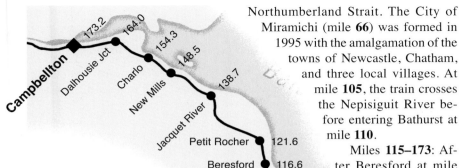

Route Highlights

Moncton to Campbellton
Newcastle Subdivision

The Ocean departs Moncton on the CN Gort subdivision and turns north at mile **11.7** to the *New Brunswick East Coast Railway*. The *Intercolonial Railway* opened this section of line on July 1, 1876.

Miles **0–60**: This forested area features numerous rivers, such as the Coal Branch River, which is crossed first at mile **14.9** and then again at **15.6**. Adamsville (mile **18.6**) is named after Michael Adams, the province's Surveyor General from 1878 to 1883. River crossings continue with the Richibucto at mile **26**, then the Kouchibouguac at mile **34**. The tracks parallel the main street of the proud Acadian town, Rogersville, at mile **44**, and then cross the Barnaby River three times at miles **48**, **52**, and **56**. The largest river crossings of the journey occur as *The Ocean* crosses the southwest fork of the Miramichi River at mile **62** and the northwest fork at mile **63**. Just to the south, the two rivers join together and flow into the Northumberland Strait. The City of Miramichi (mile **66**) was formed in 1995 with the amalgamation of the towns of Newcastle, Chatham, and three local villages. At mile **105**, the train crosses the Nepisiguit River before entering Bathurst at mile **110**.

Miles **115–173**: After Beresford at mile **116** watch to the south for your first glimpses of the Baie des Chaleurs. Look to the north at mile **135** — the land on the other side is the Province of Quebec. The train crosses the Jacquet River at mile **139**. Located on the south bank of the Restigouche River, Campbellton (mile **173**) is an entry point to Atlantic Canada from Quebec. The bridge connecting New Brunswick and Quebec by road can be seen to the north.

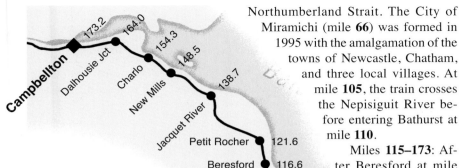

The Ocean — Contact information on page 7

17

Route Highlights

Campbellton to Riviere–du-Loup
Mont Joli Subdivision

The route you are travelling on was built between 1874 to 1876 by the *Intercolonial Railway*. It is now run by the *Matapedia Railway*.

Miles **0–12**: As you leave Campbellton, you can see Sugar Loaf Mountain to the south. The volcanic-rock mountain houses a popular provincial park featuring camping and skiing. The 47-metre (156-foot) long tunnel at mile **7** is the only tunnel on the route of *The Ocean*. At mile **12** you traverse the Restigouche River, crossing over the provincial border between New Brunswick and Quebec, as well as entering the Eastern Time zone— so adjust your travel clock and watch accordingly. Once across the river, you arrive at the town of Matapedia and a rail station that dates to 1903. Depending on the day of the week and the direction you are heading, you might join or part with VIA Rail's *Chaleur*. See page 24 for more information on this train and its route.

Miles **13–120**: The route travels through the picturesque Matapedia Valley, with the Matapedia River paralleling the route for the next 30 miles. The tracks cross the river at mile **23** and then again at miles **42** and **47**. The river has always attracted salmon fishermen, including early CPR president George Stephen, who fell in love with, and married, a local First Nations woman. From miles **53** to **56**, you can see Lac au Saumon to the east. The Amqui River is crossed at mile **60**, then the Tobogotte River at mile **64**. Lake Matapedia sits to the north be-

St Lawrence River

Montagne

St Simon 152.4

Trois Pistoles 161.7

Isle Verte 172.6

St Arsene 181.1

Riviere du Loup 188.8

tween miles **68** and **74**. During the series of rock cuts at miles **88** and **89**, look up to see an old railway flat car now used as a footbridge above the tracks. *The Ocean* crosses the Metis River at mile **102** over a 127-metre (418-foot) long bridge. Keep watching to the north for the St. Lawrence River. At mile **119** look towards the St. Lawrence near the shoreline... you may be able to catch a glimpse of a silver dome. This marks the watery grave of over one thousand people who died with the tragic sinking of *Canadian Pacific's* oceanliner *Empress of Ireland*. On a foggy night on May 21, 1914, while enroute to England, the liner was rammed by the Norwegian ship *Storstad* and sank in less than fifteen minutes.

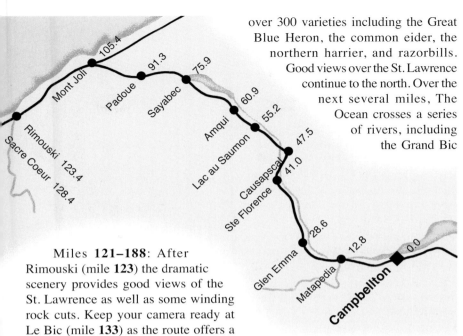

over 300 varieties including the Great Blue Heron, the common eider, the northern harrier, and razorbills. Good views over the St. Lawrence continue to the north. Over the next several miles, The Ocean crosses a series of rivers, including the Grand Bic

Miles **121–188**: After Rimouski (mile **123**) the dramatic scenery provides good views of the St. Lawrence as well as some winding rock cuts. Keep your camera ready at Le Bic (mile **133**) as the route offers a panoramic view of the bay. Bic Island can be seen 8 kilometres (5 miles) away; the opposite shore is approximately another 32 kilometres (20 miles) beyond that. The vast marine life that lives in these waters includes beluga, blue, and minke or fin whales, as well as gray seals. Birds also dominate the area, with River (mile **141**), the Renouf (mile **162**), Trois Pistoles (mile **164**), and Isle Verte River (mile **174**). The train crosses Riviere-du-Loup when passing through the city of the same name at mile **188**. At mile **190** the route returns to *Canadian National* trackage.

Morning arrival at Matapedia, Quebec, where *The Ocean* and *The Chaleur* train services separate for their respective journeys.

The Ocean — Contact information on page 7

Route Highlights
Riviere–du-Loup to Diamond Jct
Montmagny Subdivision

Miles 0–101: The train crosses the Kamouraska River at mile **26**. The community to the north, and a nearby island in the St. Lawrence, share this name, which is a First Nations word that translates to "Where the rushes are on the other side of the river." At mile **35**, *The Ocean* twice crosses the River Ouelle. Between miles **42** and **58**, you can see the Ile-aux-Coudres across the St. Lawrence, close to the north shore. The 110-metre (360-foot) long bridge at mile **59** crosses the Trois Saumon River. The majority of the names in the area derive either from First Nations translations or represent French-Canadian historical and religious figures. For example, Cap St. Ignace (mile **70**) is named after the founder of the Jesuit order, Saint Ignatius. The train continues to cross several rivers that feed into the mighty St. Lawrence, including the Bras St-Nicholas River at mile **77.5** and the River du Sud on an impressive trestle at **77.8**. Although the Montmagny subdivision does not end here, the train transfers to the Diamond Subdivision at mile **101.4**.

Riviere du Loup — 0.0
St Andre Jct — 15.3
St Pascal — 25.4
Kamouraska — 29.0
La Pocatiere Est — 41.1
La Pocatiere — 42.6
St Jean Port Joli — 56.3
Cap St Ignace — 70.5
Montmagny — 78.1
St Pierre — 82..2
St Charles — 101.3/0.0
Quebec
Carrier 8.5
Diamond 13.8
Charny 0.3

Route Highlights

Diamond Subdivision

For many years this route travelled through Levis, opposite Quebec City. Today the train bypasses Levis, continuing straight along this short 16-mile subdivision that directly connects the Montmagny Subdivision with the Drummond Subdivision. For Quebec City passengers, a shuttle bus from the Charny station provides service to the province's capital city. There is also a train from Montreal that provides direct service to Quebec City's downtown area. See page 27 for more about this route to downtown Quebec City.

View from *The Chaleur* of a quiet inlet at mile 26 on the West Chandler subdivision.

A time honoured tradition, walking at low tide to Perce Rock, is enjoyed by visitors to the resort community of Perce.

Route Highlights

Charny to Ste Rosalie
Drummondville Subdivision

Miles 8–52: The route travels away from the St. Lawrence through a region of forests that eventually gives way to large open fields. Laurier (mile **28**) is named after Canada's first French Canadian prime minister, Sir Wilfred Laurier. The train crosses the Riviere du Cheneat at mile **39** and the Little Riviere du Chene at mile **52**.

Miles **53–124:** Keep your camera ready for the high trestle above the Nicolet River, crossed first at mile **80** and then again at mile **86**. Mile **97.8** provides another photo opportunity while crossing the St. Francis River; look north to see the hydroelectric dam, before arriving at the brick Drummondville station at mile **98.3**. The train then travels through an agricultural region before reaching Ste. Rosalie at mile **125**.

Route Highlights
Ste Rosalie to Montreal
St. Hyacinthe Subdivision

Miles 40–52: After crossing a railway junction, the route joins the St. Hyacinthe subdivision at mile **40**. The delightful scenery continues as the train travels through the Richelieu Valley. One of Canada's most tragic rail accidents occurred at mile **55** on June 29, 1864. At 1:15 am, while crossing the Richelieu River, a passenger train plummeted into the water below, killing 99 people. It was later determined that the engineer was unfamiliar with the route and did not know about the signals intended to inform him of the open bridge ahead. The large unique mountains in the area were formed 125 million years ago as a result of volcanic eruptions on the bottom of what was then the Champlain Sea. Look

to the east at mile **62** to see the former St. Bruno station, now preserved as a community centre. The train stops in St. Lambert before crossing the St. Lawrence on the historic Victoria Jubilee Bridge. Construction on the

The Ocean — Contact information on page 7

Victoria Bridge began in 1854 and was completed in 1859. At first it was a single-track enclosed bridge, with only a vent running along the top for steam and smoke to escape. When the bridge became inadequate for the increasing traffic, work began in 1897 to rebuild it into a steel structure with two tracks and roads on each side; it was ready for service in December 1898. The road along the west side opened for carriages, cyclists, and pedestrians for a toll on December 1, 1899. These were the first users of the road ways, as Montreal only had one known motor vehicle. From 1909 to 1956, *Montreal and Southern Counties Railway* interurban streetcars ran along the east side of the bridge. When the St. Lawrence Seaway was opened in 1958, the south side of the bridge was split in two, permitting trains to be diverted if there is a ship in the St. Lambert lock below. Once across the 2.7-kilometre (1.7-mile) long bridge, look to the east in the middle of the road to see the large boulder known as the Irish Stone, which was unearthed during the original construction.

The stone was dedicated to the memory of immigrants who died from ship fever in 1847 and 1848. The train then travels through downtown Montreal and arrives at Central Station.

Trudel

Charny 0.0

Laurier 13.8

Fortier 28.5

Val Alain 34.4

Villeroy 40.5

Manseau 47.0

Lemieux 53.0

Daveluyville 57.6

Aston 67.6

Leonard 72.4

79.5

Perpetue 84.5

St Cyrille

For rail travellers to and from Montreal, there is nothing more convenient than the Queen Elizabeth Hotel. Located at 900 Rene Levesque Blvd. West, this classic railway hotel was originally built by *Canadian National Railways* and today is operated by Fairmont Hotels. Follow the signs in the station to the elevator that will take you up one floor to the lobby. For reservations call: 800-441-1414. Web: *www.fairmont.com*

Montreal has numerous attractions and sights to please everyone. We recommend you start in Old Montreal with a visit to the Basilique Notre Dame Cathedral. By nightfall, you'll be able to enjoy the night life along Rue St. Denis. Also plan to spend an afternoon at the Canadian Railway Museum located on the south shore of the St. Lawrence in St. Constant, a 20-minute ride from downtown. For hours, call: 450-638-1522. Web: *www.exporail.org*

Before you visit Montreal or anywhere in Quebec, you should contact Tourisme Quebec, PO Box 979, Montreal, QC H3C 2W3. Phone: 877-266-5687. Web: *www.bonjourquebec.com*

The Chaleur

VIA's *Chaleur* between Montreal and Matapedia is covered in the route of *The Ocean*. From Matapedia the route travels north along the Gaspe Peninsula, which has a long history of welcoming travellers. One of the earliest, explorer Jacques Cartier, named the Bay of Chaleur in recognition of its warm waters. If you are laying over in Matapedia, we recommend Les Motels de la Vielle Gare (the Old Station Motel). The centrepiece of this motel is the former station from Saint-Alexis, relocated today on Route 132. Reservations can be made at: 418-865-2007.

The route of *The Chaleur* travels through the Gaspe Region of Quebec. Before you leave, we suggest you contact the Gaspe Tourist Association, 357 route de la Mer, Sainte-Flavie, QC G0J 2L0. Call: 800-463-0323. Web: *www. tourisme-gaspesie.com*

Route Highlights

Matapedia to New Carlisle
Cascapedia Subdivision

In 1893 the *Baies des Chaleurs Railway* built the route between Matapedia and Caplan. Then in 1910 the *Atlantic Quebec and Western Railway* extended the line to New Carlisle. This line was part of the CN system for many years, but today it is a shortline known once again as the *Baies des Chaleurs Railway*.

Miles **0–22:** Depending on the direction you are travelling, at mile **0** in Matepedia your train will detach from or join with VIA's Oc*ean*. *The Chaleur* then travels on the north side of the Restigouche River until mile **8**, when the river ends and the Baie des Chaleurs begins. Look to the south for good views of Campbellton and Sugarloaf Mountain. It is in these waters that a fierce naval battle between the French and English took place in 1760. Timbers from one of the ships and numerous artifacts are on display at the Battle of Restigouche Museum in the town of Pointe-a-la-Croix, which can be seen to the south at mile **12.**

Miles **23–98:** You'll continue to see fantastic views to the south, over the bay, between miles **23** and **26**. After crossing the Nouvelle River (mile **33**), keep your camera ready at mile **42** where the route of *The Chaleur* passes under the highway and skirts the bay high on a cliff. After this preview, the route heads back inland from miles **45** to **47**. The building on the side of Mount St. Joseph is a shrine revering the Virgin Mary. At mile **53**, you can see Mount Maria ahead. The train crosses the Cascapedia

River at mile **60** and then the Little Cascapedia River at mile **68**. *The Chaleur* emerges from the forest for more fantastic views over the red cliffs high above the bay. As the route crosses a ravine over the Watt Brook at mile **80.9**, look down to see a small secluded beach. After crossing the Roseau Brook at mile **82**, *The Chaleur* again travels away from the coast through a region of forests and farms. At mile **90** the train crosses the wide Bonaventure River over a 108-metre (355-foot) bridge. Good views over the water continue before *The Chaleur* arrives in New Carlisle at mile **98**.

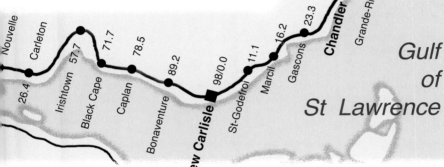

Route Highlights

New Carlisle to Chandler East
West Chandler Subdivision

The *Atlantic Quebec and Western Railway* built the remainder of the line to Gaspe, opening it for service in July 1912.

Miles **0–48**: For the first three miles, the route climbs the cliffs along the shoreline and then returns to the forest. The Shigawake River is crossed at mile **13**. After descending to sea level, *The Chaleur* crosses the north Port Daniel River at mile **22**, and then enters the town of Port Daniel where there are good views to the south of Port Daniel Bay. The tracks then climb through town, entering the only tunnel on the route at mile **23.7**. Carved out of limestone, the tunnel is 192-metres (630-feet) long. Once the train leaves the tunnel, look down to the waves crashing onto the shoreline at the bottom of the cliff. Keep your camera ready at mile **26** as the tracks cross a trestle above a wharf; this wharf is in a protected inlet and is used by local fishing boats. After Gascons at mile **28**, the train crosses the Chouinard River (mile **29.8**) and Perry Brook (mile **32.8**). After crossing the Grand Pabos River at mile **42**, the route parallels a beach on the ocean side before reaching the Chandler station at mile **44**.

Route Highlights

Chandler East to Gaspe
East Chandler Subdivision

Starting at East Chandler, the *Gaspesie Railway Corporation* operates the remaining 56 miles of track.

Miles **48–104:** It is obvious that many of the inhabitants of the area make a living from the sea. From the train you can see the lobster traps and long cod-drying tables on the properties along the tracks. After crossing the Little Pabos River at mile **50.7**, *The Chaleur* crosses the Grand River over a 209-metre (685-feet) bridge at mile **52**. Although the Perce station is at mile **55.1**, the town itself is a couple of miles away on the coast. Cabs and hotel buses pick up passengers at the station for this popular resort town. Bonaventure Island comes into view at mile **62**. At mile **65.5** a trestle crosses the L'Anse-a-Beaufils River, and then the track turns inland to avoid the coastal mountains of Mont Sainte Anne and Mont Blanc. The route descends after this, emerging from the forest at sea level at mile **74**. A causeway cuts across the bay starting at mile **75**. This large saltwater marsh created by the causeway that the tracks are situated on offers good bird watching along one of the longest beaches in the area. The marsh ends at mile **78.7** where the route crosses a bridge that releases the trapped water of the Malbaie River. Have your camera ready when the tracks return to the mainland. The route turns east briefly for the Barachois station at mile **79**. To the south is the area's largest attraction, Perce Rock; it is an 18-metre wide by 30-metre high (60 by 100 feet) natural arch. The town of Prevel was originally known as Fort Prevel and featured heavy artillery aimed toward the Atlantic during the Second World War. The railway track passes the community's golf course at mile **86**. Mile **89.8** offers a great opportunity to photograph your train on the curved trestle over the L'Anse-a-Brillant River. At mile **91**, you can see excellent views over Gaspe Bay to Forillon National Park on the opposite shore. Douglastown (mile **95**) is named after its surveyor, John Douglas. The town was a project of the English government to create a model Loyalist community. Another railway causeway, with sandy beaches on both sides, is crossed at mile **96.0**. The bridge at mile **97.6** spans the gap that releases water from the St. Jean River. The train passes a boat yard to the north at mile **102**, arriving at the station, and the end of the line opposite the Gaspe Marina, at mile **104**.

It is believed that the word "Gaspe" comes from the MicMac word that translates to "land's end." The line was built in the hope that a grain elevator would be erected to load ocean-going vessels. This did not come about, however, and the end of the line is simply a track stop a short distance from the station. Visitors who wish to explore the area should rent a car and visit Forillon National Park or the Musee de la Gaspesie located at 80 boul. Gaspe. Here you can learn more about the people of the region, Jacques Cartier's explorations in the area, and see a replica of the cross he raised in 1534. Travellers to Perce will enjoy numerous activities and attractions. Choices include taking a boat to Bonaventure Island, a visit to the gannet colony to view over 70,000 birds of this species, or a trip to some of the numerous shops to find that perfect souvenir. There is also the time-honoured tradition of walking to the famous Perce Rock at low tide. For an outstanding view and a good night's sleep, we recommend the Hotel Bonaventure located at No. 261 on Route 132. For reservations, call: 800-463-4212.

The Chaleur— Contact information on page 7

Quebec City Turn

The route across the St. Lawrence into Quebec City is the northern-most destination of the Windsor-Quebec City Corridor trains. Many trains from Montreal travel the same route of *The Ocean*, featured on page 12.

Miles 0–15.9: Charny station, on the south shore of the St. Lawrence, is located at mile **0.3** and is the start of the short remaining journey into Quebec City. As the train leaves the station, it passes through the town of Charny. On the high approach to the St. Lawrence, the tracks cross the Chaudiere River and the Trans-Canada Highway. To the west are the circular on and off ramps where the Robert Cliche Highway intersects with the Trans-Canada. The train enters the impressive Quebec Bridge at mile **1**. Keep your camera ready for great views of the river on both sides and Quebec City to the east. Once over the bridge, the tracks turn west, parallel to the river, and stop at Sainte-Foy station at mile **3.6**. The train continues to travel west until mile **4.4**, when the route turns northeast. At mile **6** the train starts travelling east along a ridge. For the next couple of miles the train descends through an industrial area. At mile **10** the train crosses the *Canadian Pacific Railway* and the Saint-Charles River at mile **11**. The train continues east and passes by Exposition Park to the south, which features a horseracing track, the Hippodrome, and the large hockey rink, Le Colisee. The route then turns to the south and heads toward the historic walled city of Quebec. Finally, you once again cross the now-wider St. Charles River before arriving at the stately Gare du Palais station at mile

15.9. This beautiful station, with its glazed brick construction, should be thoroughly admired.

Upon leaving the station, climb the hill and enjoy the cobblestones and Old World feel of the provincial capital. Not to be missed is the large Parc des Champs-de-Bataille, also known as the Plains of Abraham. To the east of here is the Citadelle, open daily from May to September, and featuring the best views of the city atop Cape Diamond. For a memorable stay in the provincial capital, we highly recommend the classic railway hotel Le Chateau Frontenac, which dominates the city skyline at 1 Rue des Carriers. Operated by Fairmont Hotels, reservations can be made at: 800-441-1414. Web: *www.fairmont.com*

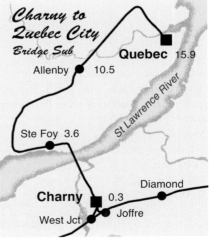

The Saguenay

ravel through northern Quebec provides views of every conceivable terrain, from fertile agricultural regions to grand valley crossings, and from countless lakes to large forests. VIA Rail Canada's *Abitibi* and *Saguenay* share the same route from Montreal to Hervey Junction. Then *The Saguenay* continues north to Jonquiere/Chicoutimi and *The Abitibi* east to Senneterre.

For travellers arriving in or departing from Montreal, we recommend staying at the Queen Elizabeth Hotel, located directly above Central Station. Our journey on the Montreal subdivision begins with mile **0** to **8.4**, which is detailed on the *Corridor* route on page 39. Both the St. Laurent and the Joliette subdivisions connect with Montreal from the east, so the mile numbering starts at the opposite end of the line. This means, for the first two subdivisions, the mileage in this guide will be listed in descending order.

Route Highlights

Taschereau Yard to Pointe-aux-Trembles
St. Laurent Subdivision

Miles 146–127: As the train leaves the *Corridor* route, it turns north through a limestone ridge and travels through the middle of Montreal's two largest railway yards: *Canadian National's* Taschereau yard to the west and *Canadian Pacific's* Cote St. Luc yards to the east. Once clear of the railway yards, the route continues through the city's

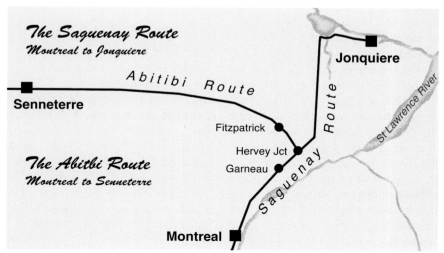

The Saguenay Route
Montreal to Jonquiere

Abitibi Route

Jonquiere

Senneterre

Fitzpatrick

Route

Hervey Jct

Garneau

Saguenay Route

St Lawrence River

The Abitbi Route
Montreal to Senneterre

Montreal

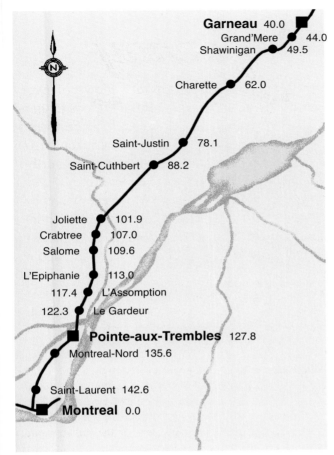

Garneau 40.0
Grand'Mere 44.0
Shawinigan 49.5
Charette 62.0
Saint-Justin 78.1
Saint-Cuthbert 88.2
Joliette 101.9
Crabtree 107.0
Salome 109.6
L'Epiphanie 113.0
117.4 L'Assomption
122.3 Le Gardeur
Pointe-aux-Trembles 127.8
Montreal-Nord 135.6
Saint-Laurent 142.6
Montreal 0.0

through the mountain began in 1912 and was completed six years later. The box-cab electric locomotives purchased by *Canadian Northern* to haul the trains were still being used (although re-powered) until a ceremonial last run on June 2, 1995. Today one of these units (with steel wheels that have wooden spokes) sits as a tribute at the Deux-Montagnes station at the northern end of the commuter line.

As you approach Pointe-aux-Trembles, mile **127.8**, you can tell how much the locals love to swim by the number of homes with a pool in their backyards.

suburbs, with Mount Royal dominating the view to the east and the green dome of the St. Joseph Oratory in the foreground. The train crosses the Deux-Montagnes subdivision at mile **141**; watch for the modern silver trains that carry commuters between downtown Montreal and the suburbs northwest of this island city. The *Canadian Pacific Railway* and *Grand Trunk* already had stations in the heart of the city. When the *Canadian Northern Railway* chose an original route to the city centre that did not infringe on its competitors' lines, it had to overcome a major obstacle: the 207-metre (679-foot) high Mount Royal. Construction of a tunnel

Route Highlights
Pointe-aux-Trembles to Garneau
Joliette Subdivision

Miles 127–88: The train leaves the island of Montreal at mile **125**, crossing the Riviere des Prairies over a 431-metre (1,416-feet) bridge, a small island, and then a second bridge over the same river. Once across, the community of Le Gardeur continues the urban sprawl of Montreal. At mile **121** the suburbs give way to more picturesque fields. At mile **106** the train crosses the Lac Quareau

A group awaits the arrival of the combined northern Quebec trains, *The Abitibi* and *The Saguenay*, at Hervey Junction, Quebec.

River over a 149-metre (490-feet) bridge, 17-metres (55-feet) above the water. Look to the north to see a small hydroelectric facility at Crabtree. At mile **101** the St. Lawrence River can be seen to the south, while at mile **98** the Laurentian Mountains start to come into view to the north. The 76-metre (250-foot) bridge at mile **87** crosses the Chicot River.

Miles **88–40:** Before an earthquake in the seventeenth century, the Maskinonge River flowed in this now-dry riverbed crossed at mile **87**. Keep your camera ready at mile **76** for the impressive 326-metre (1,071-foot) trestle crossing the river's new route 40-metres (130-feet) below. As you cross the trestle, watch for Sainte Ursule Falls on the opposite shore, close to the bridge. Once across the bridge, keep watching for the white water of the falls at the top. At mile **65** the tracks cross the Riviere du Loup with miniature whirlpools seen from both sides of the

train. The tracks cut right through the middle of the picturesque town of Charette (mile **62**). The East Yamachiche River is located in the bog crossed at mile **58**. At mile **56** the Cite de l'Energie tower in Shawinigan comes into view. The Lawrence Valley is crossed next at mile **52** before the train enters a 186-metre (610-foot) tunnel at mile **50**. Once the train emerges from the tunnel, it crosses the Shawinigan River. The town of the same name can be clearly seen to the south, and is the home of Canada's 20th prime minister, Jean Chretien. At the station one can see the wide St. Maurice River at the bottom of the hill. At mile **43** before and during the crossing of the St. Maurice, look to the north for good views of the Grand Mere hydroelectric facility. The route swings north at mile **42**, allowing for views of the opposite side of the dam. Finally, the train pulls into the large railway yards in Garneau at mile **40**.

The Saguenay — Contact information on page 7

Route Highlights

Garneau Yard to Jonquiere
Lac St. Jean Subdivision

Miles 0–46: As the train continues through this agricultural region, note the white grain silo with the red roof to the

Chambord ● 159.6
Blackburn ● 155.0
Saint-Andre ● 141.3
125.1 ● Lac-Long
116.0 ● Kiskissink
110.8 ● Brooks

95.3 ● Lac Edouard

84.2 ● Pearl Lake

77.0 ● Hegadorn

61.9 ● Linton
53.4 ● Laurent
47.5 ● Talbot

39.9 ● Riviere-a-Pierre

Hervey Jct ● 18.7

Saint-Tite 7.3

■ **Garneau** 0.0

Hebertville 181.4
Moquin 191.0
200.0
Jonquiere

west at mile **5**; this silo has been converted to a lookout. Next, the route travels through St. Tite at mile **7**. Mile **18** brings you to Hervey Junction. Here, depending on the direction you are travelling, *The Saguenay* and *The Abitibi* trainsets will be separated or joined. (See page 33 for route details of VIA's *Abitibi*.) The route of *The Saguenay* continues north. To the west at mile **23**, Lac-aux-Sables with its sandy beaches is very popular in the summer months. You first see the Batiscan River to the east at mile **28** and then cross it at mile **30**. This shallow river, with its fast moving water, is the train's travelling companion for the next 70 miles. At mile **40**, the tracks cross Riviere-a-Pierre, and at mile **43**, the Blanche River is crossed twice.

Miles **47–105**: At mile **47**, the train enters Portneuf Provincial Park, an area known for its trout fishing. Watch for moose, bears, and birds along the route. As you move through the park, look to the west to see the rapids on the Batiscan. The train exits the provincial park at mile **58** where it crosses the Misquick River. Passing through Linton (mile **61**), look to the river to see the old bridge supports. The *Quebec and Lac St. Jean Railway*, which built this route between 1888 and 1893, connected to the *National Transcontinental Railway* at La Tuque in 1909. The connecting line was abandoned in 1949. The train crosses the Batiscan River for the last time at mile **69**. A camp that was owned by a retired telephone company employee

The route of VIA's *Saguenay* winds along the shore of Lac Edouard.

uses a phone booth sign to mark the trail, a sign out of place in the northern wilderness. The stop at mile **90.7** is to service the Triton Club, which was started in 1907. Patrons leave the train and travel by boat to the lodge, located three miles down the narrow Petite Riviere Batiscan. Watch to the east at mile **92** for the Batiscan Falls. A statue of Ava Maria on the hill to the east at mile **95** looks over the town of Lac Edouard.

Miles **106–200:** The aptly named Lake Summit (mile **106**) is the highest elevation on the Jonquiere line. While traveling through Kiskissink (mile **116**), don't be alarmed if you see a rolled up object thrown from the cab of the locomotive; it is simply the engineer throwing out the Montreal newspaper for a friend! Watch for the wave of gratitude from someone coming down the path to receive the news. Lakes and rivers continue to come into view, such as Riviere Louis Joseph at mile **126**. You get your first glimpse of Lac Saint-Jean to the north at mile **157**. *The Saguenay* then turns to the east and descends to the station at Chambord. The fantastic views across this large lake continue to the north. At mile **164**, the train crosses

the Metabetchouan River. This region is known for its blueberries and for the 256-kilometre Veloroute des Bleuets (Blueberry Bicycle Trail) that circles the entire Lac Saint-Jean alongside the railway tracks at mile **165**. The route leaves the lake behind at mile **175** and travels through a fertile valley. *The Saguenay* and *Roberval Railway* shares these tracks, and it is not uncommon to see S&RR's bright yellow locomotives. Highway 170 can be seen to the north and the Riviere aux Sables is crossed at mile **200**. At mile **201**, your journey ends at the modern Jonquiere station.

After your long day on the rails, we recommend the Holiday Inn Saguenay located at 2675 boul. du Royaume. Reservations can be made at: 800-363-3124.

Plan to spend a few days in the area exploring Lac Saint-Jean or watching whales on the majestic Saguenay Fjord. A visit to nearby Chicoutimi should begin at La Croix de Sainte-Anne. This is located on Cap Saint-Joseph, and features an outstanding view of the city. Also, at la Pulperie de Chicoutimi, you can learn more about the history of the area. Don't miss the Petite Maison Blanche, which stands as a reminder of the devastating 1996 flood. In Jonquiere, those who enjoy industrial sites should be sure to visit the Aluminum Bridge. Built in 1950, it weighs a third of similar iron bridges. It is truly a tribute to the community's largest employer and fabricator of aluminum, Alcan.

Before you visit the region, contact Tourism Saguenay—Lac Saint Jean, 198 Racine Street East, Suite 210, Chicoutimi, QC G7H 1R9. Phone: 800-463-9651. Web: *www. tourismsaguenaylacsaintjean.qc.ca*

32

The Abitibi

VIA's *Abitibi* between Montreal and Hervey Junction is covered in the route of *The Saguenay*, beginning on page 28. From Hervey Junction, the track travels west on a route built by the *National Transcontinental Railway*. This line was formed in 1903 by a unique partnership between the *Grand Trunk Railway* and the federal government, under the leadership of Prime Minister Sir Wilfred Laurier. The newly-formed *Grand Trunk Pacific Railway* agreed to build the portion of track west of Winnipeg, while the Government was to build the *National Transcontinental Railway* section to the east. To appease his own cabinet members, the Prime Minister decided to build the government's part of the railway from Moncton, New Brunswick, through Quebec City, then follow an almost straight line to Winnipeg. It was agreed that the *Grand Trunk Pacific* would lease the line from the government and would be responsible for running trains once the line was completed. In 1909, the first portion of the line, between Quebec City and Hervey Junction, opened for business. By 1913, passenger trains could travel Winnipeg to Quebec City over the new route. In 1915, financial difficulties on its western lines forced the *Grand Trunk* to renege on its agreement with the government. The western lines came under the control of the *Canadian Government Railways,* later renamed *Canadian National Railways*.

Route Highlights
Hervey Junction to Fitzpatrick
La Tuque Subdivision

Miles 71–125: Here the route to the west starts at mile **71**, Hervey Junction. Depending on the direction you are travelling, your train will join or separate from VIA's *Senneterre* train. You might get a chance to walk the platform and view this quaint country station and see the switching of your train. From Hervey, the train travels through a scenic ravine between miles **74** and **79**. It then skirts Lake Masketsi to the west, starting at mile **82**. The large red-roofed lodge on the opposite side of the lake, seen at mile **84**, was believed to be a favourite destination of former Quebec premier Maurice Duplessis. The lake ends at mile **86.5**. The Bessone River widens to form a lake, seen to the east at mile **89**. Keep your camera ready when the train crosses the Riviere du Milieu at mile **95.6**. This is the highest trestle in the province crossed by a passenger train. Good views continue to the east as the train clears a small rock cut and then continues to wind around small lakes in

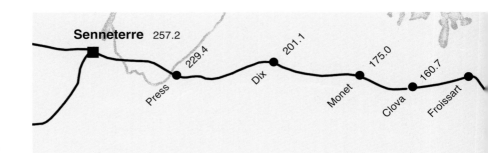

Senneterre 257.2 · Press 229.4 · Dix 201.1 · Monet · Clova 175.0 · Froissart 160.7

a forested area. La Tuque (mile **122**) derives its name from a First Nations word for "wool hat," an apt description of the rock in the middle of the Saint Maurice River. This rock was removed when a dam was built on the same site years later. A popular destination for adventure cyclists, La Tuque has a 12-kilometre circuit that starts at Parc des Chutes de la Petite Riviere Bostonnais and finishes at the municipal park. The town is also home to popular folk singer, Felix Leclerc. As you leave La Tuque, look to top of the hill to the east where you can see lumber cars waiting to be loaded with freshly-cut forest products. The train crosses the Saint Maurice River at mile **123** before entering Fitzpatrick.

Route Highlights
Fitzpatrick to Senneterre
St. Maurice Subdivision

When it was built, the line was made up of two subdivisions. Construction from Fitzpatrick on the Manouan Subdivision started in 1910, reached Parent in 1912, continued on the Oskelaneo Subdivision, and reached Senneterre in 1913.

Miles **1–36**: Fitzpatrick, named after former Quebec Lieutenant Governor Charles Fitzpatrick, was a little village that grew with the coming of the railway. The train crosses the Saint Maurice River again at mile **1**. The views of the river continue for the next few miles, before being interrupted by a short tunnel at mile **6**. Look toward the river at mile **7** to see the top of Beaumont Dam. The river is crossed one more time at mile **10** and can be seen from the north side of the train until mile **16**. At mile **18.4** a high trestle crosses the Vermilion River. At mile **20** you'll find Rapide-Blanc. With its collection of trailers at the end of a bumpy winding road, it is a destination for only the bravest of motorists. Dercy Lake can be seen to the north between miles **27** and **29**. Duplessis Lodge (mile **34**) is a popular outfitter. The two-storey building close to the tracks is a good example of a typical sectionmen's house. It was built by the *National Transcontinental Railway* from a standard plan used by the *Grand Trunk Pacific Railway*.

Miles **37–80**: McTavis (mile **38**) features some popular fishing lodges. Note the attractive log chalet on the north side of the tracks. At mile **39**, *The Abitibi* proceeds first over a trestle and then a causeway that divides the wide River Flamond. This land cruise ends at mile **43.5**. If you have any film left, there's a photo opportunity to the north at mile **45.8**: the Rapides des Coeur (Heart

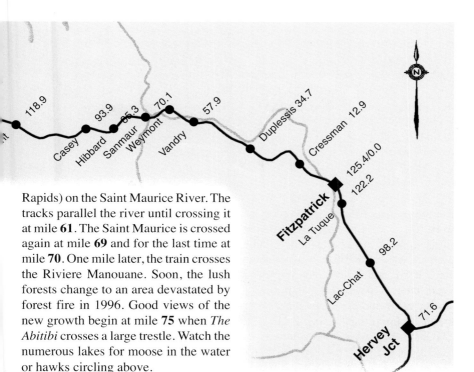

Rapids) on the Saint Maurice River. The tracks parallel the river until crossing it at mile **61**. The Saint Maurice is crossed again at mile **69** and for the last time at mile **70**. One mile later, the train crosses the Riviere Manouane. Soon, the lush forests change to an area devastated by forest fire in 1996. Good views of the new growth begin at mile **75** when *The Abitibi* crosses a large trestle. Watch the numerous lakes for moose in the water or hawks circling above.

Miles **80–190**: The burnt-out area ends at mile **81**. The route now winds through the Quebec wilderness featuring small trees, marshy areas, and sandy soil. The tracks cut through another lake at mile **100**. Letondal Lake comes into view to the south at mile **103** and can be seen until mile **105**. Sisco Mines has a mica loading facility here; piles of this shiny rock can be seen along the right-of-way. At mile **117**, the train crosses the Bazin River, a popular destination for canoe-camping excursions. A local tourist attraction is the now-shut-down dam and its power station. Once across the river, you arrive in Parent, named after Simon-Napoleon Parent, a one-time mayor of Quebec City and a provincial Premier. Look to the north for the building with the tall narrow tower. This heritage building is both the town hall and the fire hall; the tower is used for spotting fires and drying the

VIA's *Abitibi* travels high above a ravine in the Laurentian mountains.

hoses. At mile **118**, you arrive at Parent's basic white brick station. For good views of the area, visitors should visit Radar Mountain, named after a radar base that has since been dismantled. It is 8 kilometres (5 miles) out of town. From the lookout point on top of the mountain, you can see over 20 kilometres (12 miles) on a clear day. In the winter, Parent is also an important part of the region's snowmobile circuit.

As you leave the town, you can see a large wood-chip loading facility at mile **120**. Mile **130** brings you to another scorched landscape, this one from a 1995 forest fire. Though you cannot see it, the burnt-out area extends up to 16 kilometres (10 miles) from the tracks to the north and south. A microwave tower can be seen in the distance at mile **138**. The cabin at mile **148** looks out-of-place in the new growth; it was saved from the fire after being covered with a fire retardant foam. The fire district ends at mile **152** when the train crosses Lake Oskelaneo. Look to the north, on the west side of the lake, to see the Oskelaneo Outfitters camp.

The Clova station at mile **160** has long been the jump-off point for many people who travel to this remote region to try their luck at fishing its many waterways. At mile **165** the train leaves the St. Maurice region and enters the Abitibi-Temiscamingue region. Although not readily apparent, you have reached the highest elevation of your trip. Until this point, all the rivers crossed by the train flowed south to the St. Lawrence; now, the waters flow north to Hudson Bay. The Abitibi-Temiscamingue region is rich with minerals; it is quite common to see freight trains full of copper and zinc destined for Montreal. At mile **175** is another popular outfitter, Monet. To supplement facilities at the nearby Duplessis Lodge, a former *National Transcontinental Railway* crew shack is now used for accommodations, and can be seen to the south. A good opportunity to photograph your train presents itself at mile **186** as the route cuts through the middle of Serpent Lake.

Miles **191–257:** Here the forest is thick with fir trees; watch for bears that live in this northern wilderness. At mile **196** you get a good view over the trees while crossing a trestle. The siding at Dix is reached at mile **200**. The train crosses the winding Assup River at mile **216**; don't worry if you miss it, because you see it at again at mile **219** and, for the last time, from a high bridge at mile **224**. Keep your camera ready at mile **233** for the swift-flowing Megiscane River. Because of the stunted-growth fir trees at mile **235**, mountains can be seen to the north. These trees and marshes continue along the route, as does a Megiscane feeder river that is crossed at mile **243**. The train crosses the Megiscane once again at mile **253**. The train enters Senneterre after crossing the Bell River at mile **256** and then passes under Highway 113 before coming to a stop at the two-storey brick station.

This entrance to the Abitibi region is named after Lieutenant de Senneterre who helped Montcalm defend New France in 1750. The town was created with the arrival of the railway. Today the main economy is based on the forest industry, a link that is celebrated every July with the "Festival Forestier de Senneterre"

After a long day's journey, we recommend the Motel Senabi located on 7th Avenue. Reservations can be made at: 819-737-2327 or e-mailing them at: *motel.senabi@sympatico.ca*

Labrador Route

A **journey** on the *Quebec North Shore and Labrador Railway* takes travellers through a land of impressive beauty and vast mineral resources. The railway was built to transport ore from the vast reserves in the north to ocean-going vessels at Sept Isles to the south, where it is loaded onto ships and taken away for processing.

We recommend you book your tickets well in advance by contacting Vacances Inter, 451 Arnaud St., Sept-Iles, QC G4R 3B3 or by calling: 418-962-941. To learn more about iron ore mining in the area, visit the Iron Ore Company website at: *www.ironore.ca*

Route Highlights

Sept-Isles to Ross Bay Junction
Wacouna Subdivision

Miles 3.5–69: Arrive at the Sept-Isles station early and give yourself a chance to examine the two steam locomotives, No. 48 and No. 702. Once out of Sept-Isles, the rugged beauty begins at mile **10**, where a receding glacier left the rock formations found here. At mile **11.5** the train enters a 667-metre (2,197-foot) long tunnel. Keep your camera ready—once clear of the tunnel you cross a 275-metre (900-foot) long bridge high above the Moisie River. For the next 15 miles the route offers fantastic views as it snakes along the cliffs beside the river. The junction of the Moisie and Nipisso rivers (mile **28**) is popular with sport fishermen in the summer months. Many people leave the train here to try their luck in the region's rivers, which are full of salmon. Watch between miles **46** and **54** for water-

falls along the route. The breath-taking scenery continues as the train climbs the region's mountains. The winding route provides many good opportunities to photograph your entire train. The train climbs high above the Wacouno River, offering the best view to the west at mile **64**. The train enters another tunnel at mile **65**—now would be the time for those who are squeamish about heights to close their blinds! As the train emerges from the 305-metre (1,000-foot) long tunnel, look west to see the stands of black forest spruce, the bluffs, and a drop of over 213-metres (700-feet) to the river below. Then, at mile **68.6** to the west, you see the most spectacular highlight of the route, the 61-metre (200-foot) tall Tonkas Falls.

Miles 70–224: Watch for the rapids on the Wacouno River between miles **77** and **85**. The gravel pit passed at mile **84** supplies the majority of ballast for the route. Soon, the terrain changes from mountains to rolling

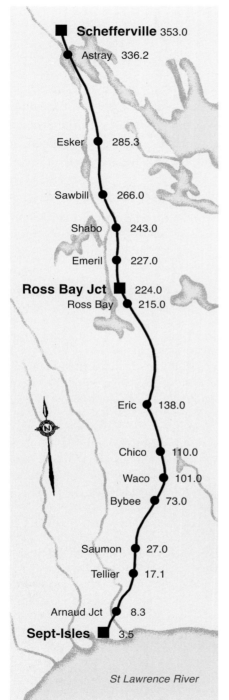

Schefferville 353.0
Astray 336.2
Esker 285.3
Sawbill 266.0
Shabo 243.0
Emeril 227.0
Ross Bay Jct 224.0
Ross Bay 215.0
Eric 138.0
Chico 110.0
Waco 101.0
Bybee 73.0
Saumon 27.0
Tellier 17.1
Arnaud Jct 8.3
Sept-Isles 3.5

St Lawrence River

hills, and from rivers to calm lakes. At mile **100**, the Wacouno River becomes Wacouno Lake and parallels the tracks for the next 30 kilometres (18 miles). The railway's highest point is at the Quebec/Labrador border at mile **148.8**. Prior to this point, all the water routes the train had passed flowed toward the St. Lawrence; now they flow north to the Labrador Sea. At Ross Bay Junction (mile **224**), your train will be met by another train to carry passengers over the thirty-mile route into Labrador City.

Route Highlights

Ross Bay Junction to Schefferville
Menihek Subdivision

Miles 224–357: The landscape of lakes and rolling hills continues, but the trees are now stunted because of the short growing season. The tracks now travel atop muskeg. This area is home to thousands of caribou. At mile **329.5** the route crosses the impressive Menihek Dam. Schefferville can be clearly seen on the opposite shore of Knob Lake, at mile **354**. You arrive at your final destination, the Schefferville station, mile **357**.

All aboard for Schefferville.

Iron Ore Company photo

Corridor Route

The current rail route between Montreal and Toronto is almost the same as when the first track was laid in 1855. Previously, travellers made the journey by steamboat or stagecoach. Once able to take the trip by rail, they rode basic wooden coaches pulled by steam locomotives. Now we have comfortable coaches with at-your-seat service on trains pulled by powerful high-speed diesel locomotives. How would travellers from then compare their all-day rail journey to today's four and a half-hours? Passengers have changed a great deal as well. Today's travellers are busy with laptop computers or cellular phones while enjoying some of the same views as the early railway passengers.

For rail travellers arriving in Montreal, the Queen Elizabeth Hotel is located at 900 Rene Levesque Blvd. West, and is managed by Fairmont Hotels. Reservations can be made at: 800-441-1414. Web: *www.fairmont.com*

Montreal, with its numerous attractions and sights, has something for everyone. Want to learn more about Canada's rail heritage? Visit the Exporail project at the Canadian Railway Museum, located a 20-minute ride from downtown on the south shore of the St. Lawrence in Delson/St-Constant. Phone: 450-638-1522. Web: *www.exporail.org*

Before you visit Montreal or anywhere in Quebec, we suggest you contact Tourisme Quebec, PO Box 979, Montreal, QC H3C 2W3. Phone: 877-266-5687. Web: *www.bonjourquebec.com*

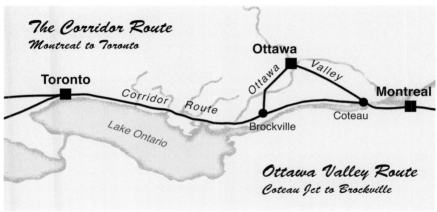

The Corridor Route
Montreal to Toronto

Ottawa

Toronto

Corridor Route

Ottawa Valley

Montreal

Coteau

Brockville

Lake Ontario

Ottawa Valley Route
Coteau Jct to Brockville

Route Highlights
Montreal to Dorval
Montreal Subdivision

Miles 0.2–9: Central Station is located in the middle of Montreal's downtown. The Bell Ampitheatre skyscraper can be seen to the west of the station. Try to catch a glimpse of the green dome behind it, which belongs to the Mary Queen of the World Cathedral. Leaving the station, the tracks

past busy highways at mile **5** and, while moving under the confusing network of freeway exits, passes through a man-made tunnel at mile **6**. The entrance to CN's Taschereau yard is passed at mile **8.7**. This is where VIA's northern Quebec trains turn north (page 28).

Crysler 83.
Morrisburg
Galop
Prescott
102.9
Brokem
Maitland
113.8
Brockville
Perth
118.0
Lyn
122.0
125.6
125.8
127.0
USA
Mallorytown
128.4
Gananoque
Leeds
Kings
152.3
156.9
162.0
174.9
Queens
Kingston
176.0
Ernestown
Bath
187.7
190.8

Lake Ontario

run under Place Bonaventure north-south for a short distance, paralleling Bonaventure Highway to the east. Once the route turns to the west, look north for the historic *Canadian Pacific Railway* Windsor Station, identified by its stone construction and tower. Behind it, atop the former station concourse, sits the Molson Centre, home of the Montreal Canadiens hockey team. The route then crosses the Lachine Canal for the first time. The tracks that travel south at mile **1.2** are the route of VIA's *Ocean* (detailed on page 12). The train travels through Pointe St. Charles, a suburb that was once home to many railway employees who worked in the large railway shops to the south. The train slips

Route Highlights
Dorval to Toronto
Kingston Subdivision

Miles 9–124: The train travels through Montreal's western suburbs, reaching Dorval at mile **10**. Here, passengers can transfer to a shuttle that takes them to Montreal's busiest airport (seen to the north). Over the next 10 miles, the train parallels the *Canadian Pacific Railway*, with its numerous commuter stations. To the south at mile **20** sits the Neil MacDonald Campus, McGill University's experimental farm site. The tracks leave the island of Montreal at mile **21.4**, crossing the Ottawa River over a 417-metre (1,370-feet) long bridge. Many Canadian explorers, such as Samuel de Champlain, Radisson, La Verendrye, and David Thompson, are

Corridor Route — Contact information on page 7

associated with this early river route. At mile **22** the route connects with Ile Perrot before crossing the river again at mile **23.9**. Once across, the scenery changes to farmers' fields and lush forests. Coteau, at mile **38**, is where the Alexandria Subdivision, the route to Ottawa, turns to the north. Riviere Beaudette is the last town in Quebec before you cross the border with Ontario at mile **45**.

Once into Ontario the town names begin to reflect the British heritage of their earliest settlers. At mile **65** the train travels a 75-kilometre (45-mile) route laid down in the 1950s as a result of the creation of the St. Lawrence Seaway. The area traversed by the original track was flooded so ocean-going vessels could reach the Great Lakes. Morrisburg (mile **92**) is home to the Upper Canada Village, created by historians who relocated and preserved buildings from the area flooded by the construction of the Seaway. Today they tell the story of how the region was settled in the early 1800s. Iroquois (mile **100**) also grew with people who were displaced by the Seaway. Look to the south to catch a glimpse of the Seaway and of the International

Bridge linking Canada and the United States. You can tell you have rejoined the original route at mile **113**, when you pass the historic Prescott station, built in the 1850s. Look to the south at mile **116.5** to see a church and a cemetery, which is the final resting place of Barbara Heck, who established Methodism in North America.

Miles **125–199**: Just before reaching Brockville at mile **125**, the rail route to Ottawa turns north. The Brockville station mural has three panels depicting the arrival of P.T. Barnum's Circus in 1877; the 1951 visit of Princess Elizabeth and the Duke of Edinburgh; and the Brockville railway tunnel. Departing the station you can look up and down Perth Street. Jon's Restaurant, seen to the south, is a favourite spot of local rail enthusiasts. The decor features photos of the area's rail history as well as offering a great view of the passing trains. The rock cut at mile **128** signals the beginning of a changing landscape; more curved rock cuts are featured at miles **131** and **132** and then at **142** and **143**. At mile **134** the small cemetery for Yonge's Mills can be seen on both sides of the tracks. Gananoque has long been a popular starting point for tourists to visit the Thousand Islands, a stretch of the St. Lawrence River noted for its numerous islands. Gananoque Junction Station at mile **154** was part of the *Thousand Islands Railway*, completed in 1883. From here, the area's shortest railway (3.3 miles/5.4 kilometres) followed the Gananoque River to the shores of the St. Lawrence. Station stops included a cemetery (fortunately, tickets for passengers were round-trip!) and a cheese factory, before reaching the St. Lawrence. The last of the route was removed in 1997; today it is a nature walk. The railway is not forgotten, however. *Thousand Islands Railway* locomotive No. 500, built in 1931, and known as the "Susie Push," is proudly displayed in Confederation Park.

The train crosses the Gananoque River at mile **155**. Watch on both sides at mile **169** for the crossing of the Rideau Canal; directly below are the Kingston Mills Locks. In total, there are 49 locks along this 202-kilometre (125-mile) water route to Ottawa. It was built after the war of 1812 by the Royal Corps of Engineers (under the supervision of Lt. Col. John By) as a strategic and secure way to move troops and supplies. At mile **172**, as you approach Kingston, look south to see the Cataraqui River as well as a quarry that undoubtedly supplied some of the limestone that helped to build some of this city's finest buildings. You can see the limestone up close at mile **173** as the train passes through a rock cut. Kingston's modern station (mile **176**) is the fourth to serve this community (the other three still survive to this day). *Grand Trunk* built both an outer and inner station, and the *Kingston and Pembroke Railway* built a station near the waterfront. Today this station is a tourist information centre, with

Canadian Pacific steam locomotive 1095 on display outside. This locomotive was built by Kingston's Canadian Locomotive Company, which built over 3000 locomotives between 1850 and 1969. Another local historic site is Bellevue House,

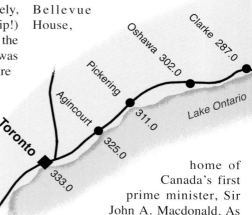

home of Canada's first prime minister, Sir John A. Macdonald. As well, Kingston houses eight correctional facilities; if you look to the south at mile **177**, you see the red roof of the Collins Bay facility.

At mile **179.8** the train curves along Collins Bay, with its popular marina. This is your first glimpse of Lake Ontario, with good views continuing towards Amherst Island to the south and the North Channel that separates it from the mainland. The old stone station at Ernestown sits quietly to the north of the tracks at mile **188**. The route turns slightly inland, away from the lake, travelling through picturesque fields and rolling hills. Keep your camera ready and pointed to the north at mile **192** where there are two large barns with concrete grain silos. The Napanee River is crossed at mile **198** on a stone viaduct built in 1856. Look to the south to see great views of Napanee and of a gristmill built by the government for loyalists who fled the American

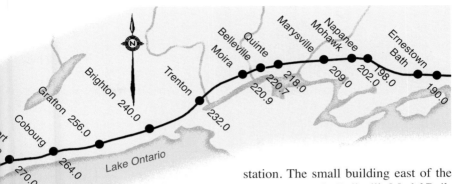

Revolution.

Napanee features another historic station at mile **199**.

Miles **200–333:** The rolling countryside continues with tree-lined fields and hobby farms. To the north at mile **209** you can see the bleachers for the Shannonville Motorcross Park. The train crosses the Salmon River at mile **212**, and then passes under the *Canadian Pacific Railway* tracks at mile **214**. The Belleville Community Airfield can be seen south of the old stone farmhouse at mile **217**. Soon, at mile **220**, the train arrives at Belleville's two-storey historic station. The small building east of the station houses the Belleville Model Railroad Club. A popular time to visit Belleville is during the annual Waterfront Festival held here each July on the shores of the Bay of Quinte. Passengers from the train get a good view of Belleville at mile **221** as the train crosses the Moira River. The community's water tower and the steeple of St. Paul's Church dominate the skyline.

Mile **232.2** finds the train crossing the Trent River. The locks seen on the west side of the river are from the Trent-Severn Canal, which connects the city of Trent with Georgian Bay on Lake Huron. At mile **232.8** you see a

Thousand Islands Railway No. 500, "The Susie Push," on display in Gananoque, Ontario.

43

A train travelling between Montreal and Toronto at Brockville station.

different set of tracks passing under the route of your train. This is the original route of the *Ontario Central Railway*, built in 1879. Today this small portion of track, to a grain elevator to the north, is all that remains of this line. The *Canadian Pacific Railway* tracks to the south are then paralleled starting at mile **234**. Although the Brighton station is no longer used by the railways, it lives on as Memory Junction, a private museum with a few pieces of rolling stock and former *Canadian National Railways* steam locomotive 2534, built in 1906.

At mile **260,** forests and orchards give way to good views of Lake Ontario to the south. Cobourg (mile **264**) houses another fine old station. The mural on the building to the south honours hometown heroine Marie Dressler, an actress in the days of silent movies. Leaving town, the route once again passes under the *Canadian Pacific Railway*. At mile **270** the train crosses the Ganaraska River on a curved trestle 375-meters (1,232-feet) long. This

bridge offers you a good opportunity to take photos of the train from either side. To the north sits the town of Port Hope, while to the south is the harbour providing shelter to numerous boats. After crossing the bridge, the train reaches Port Hope's restored stone station.

At mile **271** the route rises high above the lake, with great views to the south. Golfers on the course to the north have to be careful their ball does not end up in Ontario's largest water trap. Watch to the south at mile **274** for a nice view of this tree-filled valley, with Lake Ontario providing the backdrop. At mile **276** you can see the large smokestacks from a coal-fired power-generating station to the south. The farms and pastures continue along the route. At mile **288** we hope the train does not disturb the lawn bowlers to the north.

The train enters Oshawa at mile **297**. The McLaughlin family earned its fortune in this city through the McLaughlin Carriage Company, established in the 1800s. They wisely forsaw the future,

44

switching to the manufacture of motor vehicles. In 1918 their enterprise became General Motors of Canada. Today GM has its Canadian head office in Oshawa. The train passes the GM plant to the south at mile **300**. Look for rows of autoracks here, ready to load up the new vehicles and transport them to market. On the opposite side of the tracks at mile **302** (to the north side) is the Oshawa station. This is also the eastern terminal for Toronto's *GO Transit* commuter trains. The Pickering nuclear power station, on the shore of Lake Ontario, rises in the distance at mile **313**. The train crosses the Rouge River at mile **316** and skirts the shore as it enters a more urban setting. From the GO station in Scarborough (mile **325**), watch for your first glimpses of Toronto's impressive CN Tower. Evidence of this sprawling city is everywhere as you pass mile **330** with the Gerard Square Mall to the south and a Toronto Transit Commission subway system maintenance centre to the north. The tracks cross the Don River at mile **331** and then spend the next two miles navigating the trackage into Toronto's Union Station. The former Gooderham & Worts Distillery is now the popular "Distillery District" tourist attraction. Watch to the southwest for the CN Tower and Skydome. Before entering the station, you can look along Toronto's famous Yonge Street to the north. You reach the trainshed for Toronto's Union Station at mile **333**.

For rail travellers to and from Toronto, the Royal York Hotel is the most convenient lodging option. Located across the street from Union Station at 100 Front Street West, rail travellers can walk across Front Street or take the tunnel connecting the station to the hotel. Managed today by Fairmont Hotels, this classic railway hotel has hosted royalty, heads of state, celebrities, and travellers from around the world since 1929. Reservations can be made at: 800-441-1414. Web: *www.fairmont.com*

Toronto has an amazing array of attractions. Close to the station, at the corner of Front and Yonge streets, sits the restored Bank of Montreal building housing the Hockey Hall of Fame. The entrance is found on the lower level of BCE Place next door. Young and old will enjoy the hockey memorabilia and the interactive events. Be sure to visit the great hall to see hockey's famous trophies including the Stanley Cup. Web: *www.hhof.com*. Further north, the Royal Ontario Museum features one of Canada's largest collection of artifacts and it is located at 100 Queens Park (Avenue Road at Bloor Street). Toronto's own castle, Casa Loma (1 Austin Terrace) was the vision of millionaire Sir Henry Pellat; it is open to all today. To learn more about the area before Toronto became Canada's largest city, visit Fort York and experience the defense of the Fort in 1812. Of course, you can see all of this from the 553-metre (1815-foot) CN Tower. Visitors to the world's tallest free-standing structure can enjoy the view from the Observation Level, and those who want to go even higher can travel another 100 metres to the Skypod Level. When you are done looking at the distant horizon, look straight down to see trains departing Toronto's Union Station.

Before you visit Toronto, or anywhere in Ontario, we suggest you contact the Ontario Travel Information Centre, Eaton Centre, Level 1, PO Box 104, 220 Yonge Street, Toronto, ON M5B 2H1. Call: 800-ONTARIO (416-314-5900). Web: *www.ontariotravel.net*

Ottawa Valley

n **1832** settlers in the Ottawa Valley welcomed the construction of the Rideau Canal as a sign of progress. The new community was named Bytown after Lieutenant Col. John By, who oversaw the work on the canal. Soon log booms replaced the river's canoes as the forestry industry thrived. As the community's importance grew, its name was changed to Ottawa, after the local Outaouac First Nation. In 1857, Queen Victoria chose the settlement as the country's capital.

The route of VIA's *Corridor* services from Montreal to Coteau Junction is covered in the Montreal to Toronto route on page 39. From here the route turns northwest to travel to the nation's capital.

Route Highlights

Coteau Junction to Ottawa
Alexandria Subdivision

Miles 0–76: At mile **0**, the route turns northward, away from the Kingston Subdivision. The town of St. Polycarpe can be seen to the west at mile **4**. The train crosses the east-west rail route of the *Canadian Pacific's* rail line between Montreal and Toronto at mile **6**. Mile **13** marks the Quebec-Ontario border. Alexandria, at mile **23**, was originally known as Priest Mills after Father Alexander Macdonell, who built a gristmill in the area. When the town was incorporated in 1883, the name was changed to reflect the community's founder. South of the community's restored brick station is the Atlantic Hotel.

After Alexandria, the route travels through a forested area, then reaches Maxville at mile **34**. The terrain becomes dotted with scenic farms. Keep your camera ready at mile **39** for a photo of the stone church located at Moose Creek. At mile **47** the town of Casselman can be seen as the route cuts across Main Street and then crosses the wide South Nation River. The train travels through the Ottawa suburbs before reaching the Ottawa Station at mile **76.5.**

Ottawa's modern station is located in the southwest corner of the city. The Transitway bus corridor has a stop directly in front of the station; from here you can make a connection to downtown Ottawa. Downtown, across from the former Union Station you find the stately Chateau Laurier, located at 1 Rideau Street. Built by *Grand Trunk Pacific* and operated today by Fairmont Hotels, the hotel was the vision of *Grand Trunk Pacific* General Manager, Charles Melville Hays. Sadly, he perished on the ill-fated *Titanic* (which also took to the bottom of the Atlantic some furniture destined for the hotel) and never saw its official opening in 1912. Reservations can be made at: 800-441-1414. Web: *www.fairmont.com*

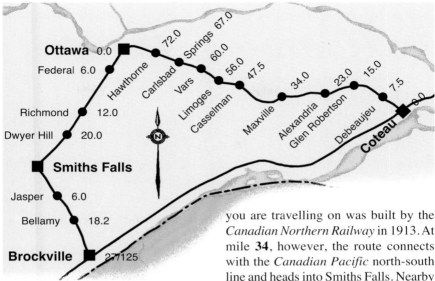

There is no shortage of attractions in Ottawa/Hull. You can find everything from the Canada Science and Technology Museum to the historic Canadian Parliament Buildings. If you are planning a visit we suggest you contact Ottawa Tourism, Suite 1800, 130 Albert St., Ottawa, ON K1P 5G4. Call: 800-465-1867. Web: *www. tourottawa.org*

The Beachburg Subdivision was built for trains to cross the southern part of Ottawa and connects the Ottawa Station to the Smiths Falls Subdivision. At mile **1** look to the north to see the Ottawa skyline. The Rideau Canal is crossed at mile **5**. Federal and the Smiths Falls Subdivision are reached at mile **6**.

Route Highlights
Federal to Smiths Falls East
Smiths Falls Subdivision

Miles 0–34: The train travels through an isolated area of farms, thick forests, and swamps. The Jock River can be seen to the east at mile **14**. Thus far, the line

you are travelling on was built by the *Canadian Northern Railway* in 1913. At mile **34**, however, the route connects with the *Canadian Pacific* north-south line and heads into Smiths Falls. Nearby is the Smiths Falls Railway Museum, which includes a restored *Canadian Northern* station.

Route Highlights
Smiths Falls to Brockville
Brockville Subdivision

Miles 0–27: After visiting the restored Smiths Falls station, those with a sweet tooth will wish they had taken a tour of the Hershey plant at mile **1**. Before crossing the Rideau Canal and River, look to the west to see the Heritage House Museum. At mile **6** the train passes through the town of Jasper. Your train will connect with the Kingston subdivision at Brockville. See page 41 to follow the route to Toronto. The *Brockville and Ottawa Railway* originally continued south to the St. Lawrence River, through Canada's first railway tunnel, which opened in 1860. It is closed today, but visitors to Brockville's waterfront can view the tunnel's South Portal.

Tecumseh Route

A **journey** through Southwestern Ontario features everything from large cities to peaceful farms. The train route visits attractive villages and towns full of charm and history, featuring some of the country's oldest and most unique railway stations.

In the 1800s, the *Great Western Railway* foresaw wealth in the region, and its supporters envisioned a railway providing endless profits. The formula was simple: build a land route for the United States, between Niagara and Windsor. This would provide a shorter, more direct route on the north side of Lake Erie for rail traffic between the American Midwest and New York State. Sod was symbolically turned on the new railway in London, Ontario, on October 23, 1849, but construction did not begin until 1851. The route between Hamilton and London opened for traffic in the closing months of 1853, and the southern portion between Windsor and Chatham opened shortly thereafter. The last link between Chatham and London was completed in 1854. With the mainline completed, the *Hamilton & Toronto Railway* was formed by the *Great Western Railway* to connect the east-west line to Toronto. The line flourished after its completion in 1855. The company achieved many Canadian railway firsts, including: the first railway mail car; the first Canadian-built sleeping cars; and the first Canadian-built locomotive with a steel boiler.

Competition between the *Great Western Railway* and the *Grand Trunk Pacific Railway* in the early 1880s was fierce. This came to an end in 1882 when the *Grand Trunk Pacific Railway* successfully took over the *Great Western* and amalgamated the line into its own system. The *Grand Trunk* later became a large part of the *Canadian National Railways* system.

Today the train to Windsor travels the original route of the *Great Western*. Many Americans travel east from Detroit to visit Canada, spending the weekend in Toronto to shop and possibly take in a show. Canadians also travel the line to visit friends and family in southwestern Ontario, or continue on to destinations in the United States.

Route Highlights

Toronto to Bayview
Oakville Subdivision

Miles 0–36: Departing Toronto's Union Station Train shed, you see the track side of the Metro Toronto Convention Centre to the north. Look south and straight up to see Toronto's most distinctive attraction, the CN Tower. Your train then passes under the John Street pedestrian walkway connecting downtown Toronto with the CN Tower and Skydome, a unique stadium featuring a retractable roof. While passing under the bridge, notice the John Street switch house, which had to lose its roof for the walkway's construction. After passing Skydome, the tracks are below the city level. Above and to the south you can see a memorial dedicated to the Chinese railway workers who helped to construct the *Canadian Pacific Railway*. Erected in 1989, the memorial is in the form of bridge girders. On the north side of the tracks sit the offices of The Globe and Mail, one of Canada's national newspapers. At mile **2**, to the south, the train passes by the Canadian National Exhibition grounds, site of Canada's largest fair held every August. Lake Ontario's Humber Bay can be seen to the south at mile **3**. To the north are more of Toronto's large condominium and apartment blocks, overlooking the lake. The Humber River is crossed at mile **5**.

The green and white bi-level cars of the GO commuter trains that service the Greater Toronto Area receive their maintenance here at mile **7**. First begun 1967, *GO Transit's* trains and buses now carry close to 40 million people a year. The train crosses Etobicoke Creek at mile **9**, passes the Port Credit station at mile **12.8**, and crosses the Port Credit River at mile **13**. Mile **17** brings you past the Windsor Salt plant to the south. The Ford Canada automotive plant complex is seen to the north at mile **19**.

VIA and *GO Transit* share the modern station at Oakville (mile **21.4**). After this stop the train crosses a 49-metre (490-foot) long bridge high above Sixteen Mile Creek. At mile **25.9** you cross Twelve Mile Creek, after which the train

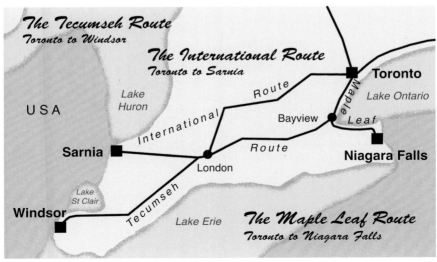

leaves the cityscape to travel through the Royal Botanical Gardens. The pedestrian bridge above the tracks at Bayview (mile **36**) is a popular spot with local rail enthusiasts. Travellers get an excellent view of the Burlington Bay to the south while the train negotiates Bayview Junction. If you are travelling to Niagara Falls, the route highlights continue on page 56.

___

Route Highlights
Bayview to London
Dundas Subdivision

Miles 0–37: For the first two miles, the train continues to travel through the lush forests of the Royal Botanical Gardens up Dundas Hill. By mile **3** the train has climbed to the top of the Niagara Escarpment. To the south you get a good view of Hamilton and the surrounding area. With the suburban setting left behind, the scenery changes to rolling hills and tree-lined farms. Watch for fox, deer, hawks, and redwing blackbirds. These small birds, the size of sparrows, are black with the exception of the bright reddish-orange marks at the shoulders of their wings. The train crosses Fairchild Creek at mile **18**.

Shortly after, the train enters Brantford and stops at the city's unique station (mile **23**). Built by the *Grand Trunk* in 1904, it is different from other stations on the route with its four-storey tower, blue granite, and dark brick construction. The red tiles on the roof each weigh seven pounds. Brantford is named after renowned native leader Joseph Brant, who sided with the British during the American Revolution. After the war he led the Six Nations band, displaced from what is now New York State, to settle in the area. One of the most popular attractions in this well-kept city is the Bell Homestead National Historic Site. Here visitors can learn more about Alexander Graham Bell and his famous first telephone call in 1874.

Get your camera ready for the bridge over the Grand River, a Canadian Heritage River, crossed at mile **29.8**. The bridge here is 233-metres (767-feet) long and 30-metres (100-feet) above the river. The view to the south features a curving waterfall and the town with its shops that back onto the river. At mile **30**, the Paris building to the north is the W.M. Kipp Funeral home, with its beige brick construction

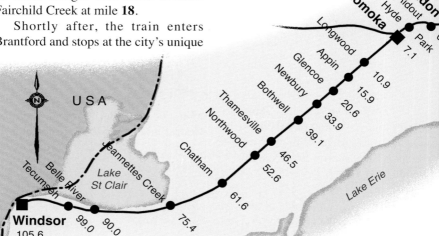

and attractive Victorian style. The terrain after Paris continues to be rolling hills and, at mile **34**, the tracks cross the Nith River. The track has long straight sections in the vicinity of Princeton at mile **37**.

Miles **38–78**: At mile **49**, the two-and-a-half storey station at Woodstock has a certain charm all its own. Built in 1853, the building stands out with its ornate fascia trim along the roof. Leaving Woodstock, the tracks travel through a picturesque valley. A Christmas tree farm can be seen to the south at mile **53**. At miles **54** and **55** the train passes abandoned quarries whose contents were used to build some of the area's noblest buildings. When arriving at Ingersoll (mile **59**),

The train travels through more of this rich agricultural region before reaching London at mile **78**.

Route Highlights
London to Komoka
Strathroy Subdivision

Miles **0–9**: First at mile **0.4**, then a mile later, the train crosses the Thames River, which winds its way through London. At mile **9**, tracks of the Strathroy subdivision proceed on the north side, towards Sarnia. The tracks to Windsor proceed on the south side.

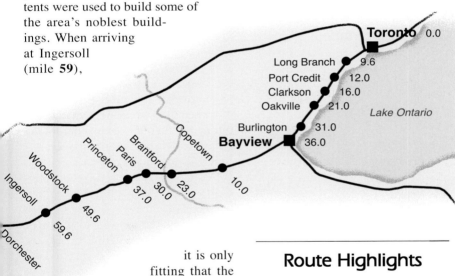

it is only fitting that the Ingersoll Cheese Co. building can be seen to the north. It was here, in 1865, that the Canadian commercial cheese industry began. In 1866, to promote the industry, a massive cheese was produced that was 6.4-metres (21-feet) round and weighed 3311.2 kilograms (7,300 pounds). It travelled to the New York State Fair and London, England, for display.

Route Highlights
Komoka to Windsor
Chatham Subdivision

Miles **0–105**: The terrain is now the flattest it has been the entire trip, with large fields and farms, many with large round concrete silos. Glencoe (mile **27**) has preserved its station and moved it a short distance from its original location. You will get your last view of the Thames River when you cross it at mile **47**. The Chatham

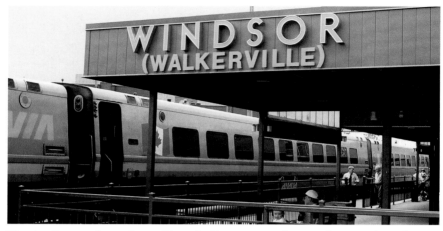

The heritage of southern Ontario lives on as the modern station sign at Windsor reflects the location of the station in the "Old Walkerville" area.

Railroad Museum (mile **61**) tells the story of the area's railway history inside a former *Canadian National* baggage car. The car, seen to the south, is in its original green and yellow colour scheme. Chatham was also a northern terminus for a different kind of railroad, the "Underground Railroad." It was here that approximately 5,000 African American slaves ended their journey to freedom between 1850 and 1861. Lake St. Clair comes into view at mile **76**. Along the lake you'll see row after row of distinctive homes and cottages where owners can drive their cars up to the front door and park their boats in the backyard waterway that connects to the lake. Good views to the north continue between miles **85** and **95**. At mile **99** the Tecumseh water tower proclaims that this is the "Home of the Green Giant."

Windsor is one of the major automobile production centres in Canada. You will see many railway automobile transport cars while travelling through the city, all ready to be loaded with new vehicles. The train arrives at the modern Windsor station (mile **105.6**), located in the middle of the Hiram Walker distillery complex. The area around the plant was originally called Walkerville; locals still use that name to refer to the area to this day. The plant is still in operation. You can learn more about taking a tour by calling: 519-561-5499. After lunch at Jackie's Variety & Lunch bar (located at Wyandotte Street and Devonshire) we recommend a stroll along Confederation Park. This is the only place in Canada where you can look to the north and see the continental United States, and the stunning Detroit skyline. In this park, you'll see where *The Great Western Railway* ferryboat Lansdowne crossed the Detroit River. Also on display is *Canadian National* locomotive No. 5588.

For more information on visiting Windsor, contact the Convention & Visitors Bureau of Windsor, Essex County & Pelee Island, 333 Riverside Drive West, Suite 103, Windsor, ON N9A 5K4. Call: 800-265-3633. Web: *www.city.windsor.on.ca*

International Route

Affectionately referred to by some railway employees as the "Back Route," the train to Sarnia travels on a line built north of the first line in southwestern Ontario. It was built by the *Grand Trunk Railway* in the 1850s to compete with the *Great Western Railway*. It reached London and a connection with the *Great Western* in 1858. VIA's service includes trains that travel between Sarnia and Toronto on a daily schedule.

Route Highlights

Toronto to Halwest
Weston Subdivision

Miles 0–17: Departing Toronto's Union Station train shed, look south and straight up to see Toronto's most distinctive attraction, the CN Tower. Your train will then pass under the John Sreet pedestrian walkway conecting downtown Toronto with the CN Tower and Skydome. At mile **6** you cross Black Creek, then pass Weston Station at mile **8**. While crossing the Humber River at mile **9.6**, you can see the Weston Golf Club to the south. At mile **13**, you can see a line of trees marking Woodbine Racetrack to the north. After this, the Lester B. Pearson International airport can be seen to the south. The route continues through suburbs and industrial areas before reaching Halwest Junction at mile **14**.

Route Highlights

Bramalea to Silver
Halton Subdivision

Miles 11–24: The Weston Subdivision connects with the Halton Subdivision at mile **11**. At one time, horse-drawn carriages would meet the train at Brampton station (mile **15**). Both the 1857 viaduct that crosses the Credit River (mile **22.5**) and the Georgetown station (mile **23.5**) were built with limestone from the area. At Silver (mile **24**) the Halton Subdivision turns southward, but your passenger train continues onto the Guelph Subdivision.

VIA Rail 6437 gets ready to depart Southern Ontario in the shadow of The Fairmont Royal York Hotel.

Route Highlights
Silver to London Junction
Guelph Subdivision

Miles 30–119: The mileage abruptly begins at mile **30**. Keep your camera ready for mile **41** when the Credit Valley over a high bridge. Entering Guelph (mile **48.5**), you cross the Speed River, before arriving at the Guelph Station. Just east of the station, you can view preserved steam locomotive 6167. The train crosses the Grand River at mile **58**. Kitchener features another historic station, on the south side of the tracks, at mile **62**. The route then varies between forested areas and large fields before crossing the Nith River at mile **75**. Stratford, famous for its yearly Shakespeare festival, is reached at mile **88**. At mile **98** stands a *Grand Trunk Western* caboose. The town of St. Marys has a water tower proclaiming it to be "A town worth living in." Its quaint brick station, with rounded corners, is reached at mile **99**. The same company that built stations along the Kingston Subdivision (Montreal to Toronto) built St. Marys Junction station. Its most famous employee, Thomas Edison, worked the night shift here in 1863. The route now turns south to connect with the Dundas Subdivision at mile **119** and the mileposts change to **76–78** as you travel through London.

Route Highlights
London to Sarnia
Strathroy Subdivision

Miles 0–58: It is only fitting that the river passing through London is called the Thames. You cross it when leaving the city, at mile **0.4**, and again at mile **1.4**. At mile **9.8** the Chatham Subdivision, the route to Windsor, peels away on the south side. Komoka Station has been moved to the nearby Community Centre grounds and makes up part of the Komoka Railway Museum. Also on display is a 1913 Shay locomotive used in logging operations, as well as a full wall of railway lanterns. In Strathroy (mile **20**), the train crosses the Sydenham River. As you depart the town, you can see large greenhouses to the north. The train passes by large fields in this rich agricultural region. Six kilometres (3.7 miles) to the south of Wyoming, visitors can learn more about early oil exploration at the Oil Museum of Canada located in Oil Springs. Sarnia's large brick station, at mile **59**, is located on the south side of the city. Freight trains continuing on to the United States, will pass through the St. Clair

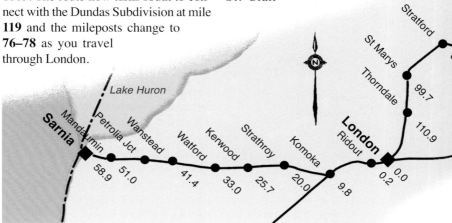

International Route — Contact information on page 7

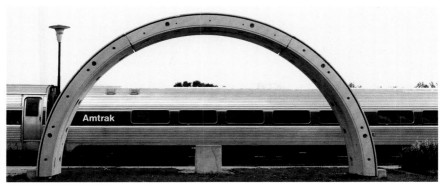

VIA Rail/Amtrak joint service *The International* seen alongside a display of the St. Clair River tunnel shield outside the Sarnia station.

Tunnel, built to eliminate the two hours it took for ferries to cross the St. Clair River. The original tunnel, constructed with cast iron tunnel shields, was completed in 1890. When the old tunnel became out-of-date for modern double-stack freight trains, CN built a new larger tunnel using the same technique, though this time it used curved concrete sections. The new tunnel, opened in 1994, parallels the old one.

North) to learn more about the community's history and to see one of Southwestern Ontario's largest model railways. Also, the Centre by the Bay, at 120 Seaway Road, features displays related to the region and an interesting displays related to the region. It also has an interesting concrete display outside depicting the entire Great Lakes system complete with flow-

Weston 8.6
Brampton
Rock Cut
Silver
15.4
24/30
Toronto 0.0
Parkdale 2.4
Mosborough
Guelph
41.7
Bresleau
48.8
Waterloo
53.9
Petersburg
58.4
Kitchener 62.0
New
Hamburg 69.0
akespeare 75.0
82.0
Lake Ontario

ing water. Also in nearby Centennial Park is *Canadian National's* locomotive 6069, a popular backdrop for wedding photos.

A sample of both the cast iron and concrete curved sections are on display outside the station.

If you are planning a visit to Sarnia, we recommend a visit to the Discovery House Museum (475 Christina Street

For more information on visiting Sarnia, we recommend that you contact the Visitors Bureau of Sarnia/Lambton, 556 North Christina Street, Sarnia, ON N7T 5W6. Call:519-336-3278. Web: *www.city.sarnia.on.ca*

The Maple Leaf

With Lake Ontario to the North and Lake Erie to the South, the Niagara Peninsula has a very distinctive regional character. Rail services through the region include VIA's daily service to Niagara Falls and an Amtrak train that operates between Toronto and New York City. The trip begins at Toronto's Union Station on the Oakville Subdivision, which is detailed on page 49. After Bayview Junction, the tracks turn to the south. Look to the east for good views of Burlington Bay and the Skyway Bridge in the distance. To the west is the first lock of the short-lived Desjardin's Canal.

The Grimsby Subdivision begins in Niagara Falls, so the mileposts work in reverse.

Route Highlights

Hamilton to Niagara
Grimsby Subdivision

Miles 43–0: With the Hamilton downtown area to the south, the train proceeds through the large Dofasco and Stelco industrial plant sites. Those employees are the source of Hamilton's nickname, "Steeltown." The Niagara Escarpment can be clearly seen to the south at mile **34**, and will be visible for the next few miles. Grimsby (mile **27**) once had a large brick station that was destroyed by fire. An earlier wooden station to the south still exists today as a builder's second-hand supply store and curio shop. You are now in the heart of Ontario's "Wine Country," as evidenced by the numerous vineyards passed during the next few miles. The climate is also perfect for growing produce— watch for cherry, apple, and peach trees in the fields along the track. Rock quarried from the Beamsville area (mile **23**) was used in the supports of the Victoria

Maple Leaf Route — Contact information on page 7

Jubilee Bridge crossing the St. Lawrence River at Montreal and in the original Sarnia railway tunnel under the St. Clair River. Keep watching to the north over Lake Ontario: on a clear day you should be able to see the CN Tower looming over the Toronto skyline. At mile **17** you cross Twenty-Mile Creek, where you can see the supports of a previous railway bridge. Strangely, you cross Sixteen-Mile Creek at mile **15**. A good time to visit St. Catharines (mile **11**) is in September for the Niagara Grape and Wine Festival. After departing the St. Catharines station, you get a good view of the city centre to the south while crossing the bridge high above the Twelve-Mile Creek. There have been four successive Welland Canals that provide passage for ships between Lake Ontario and Lake Erie. The train crosses the first, completed in 1829, at mile **9.9**. Then the route passes over the present canal, completed in 1932, on a drawbridge at mile **8.5**. Look to the south to see the large gates of Lock Number 4. The 1840s canal is passed at mile **7.7**. At mile **2**, you cross yet another waterway, this one carrying water diverted from the Upper Niagara River to the Queenstown Power Plant eight miles away. The train arrives at the Niagara Falls station at mile **0**. For those passengers continuing on to the U.S. after departing the station, the train passes high above the Niagara River, which marks the Canada/United States border.

Whether you are visiting the area to see the magnificent falls or to enjoy the variety of activities on Clifton Hill, we recommend the Hampton Inn, north of the Falls at 4357 River Road, a short distance from the train station. Reservations can be made at: 800-465-6027. Web: *www.niagarafallshamptoninn.com*

The large station in Niagara Falls greets passengers enroute to the famous waterfalls from which the community gets its name.

The Northlander

To promote settlement and to encourage economic activity in Northern Ontario, the provincial government formed the *Temiskaming and Northern Ontario Railway*. The potential of the line was revealed when railway construction uncovered reserves of silver and cobalt in the area of Long Lake. With the boom on, it was decided to continue building north to meet the route of the new east-west line of the *National Transcontinental Railway*, then under construction, in a location later named Cochrane. To reflect the railway's changing mandate, the name was changed in 1948 to the *Ontario Northland Railway*. To learn more, or to make reservations, contact them at 555 Oak Street East, North Bay, ON P1B 8L3. Call: 800-461-8558. Web: *www.northlander.com*. Tickets can also be purchased on the east side of Toronto's Union Station Grand Hall at the Paper Depot sales counter.

The Northlander travels north from Toronto on the *Canadian National* Bala Subdivision, detailed on the route of *The Canadian* (see pages 73–74) and continues north of Washago on the Newmarket Subdivision, starting at mile **88.**

Route Highlights

Washago to North Bay
Newmarket Subdivision

Miles 88–227: After departing Washago (mile **88.9**), the train arrives at Gravenhurst at mile **112**. Keep your camera ready at mile **118** for the Hawk Rock Viaduct, and again at mile **121**, where first the south branch and then the north branch of the Muskoka River are crossed before passing through Bracebridge. Huntsville (mile **146**) once featured a unique narrow gauge railway, which was less than two miles in length. The railway bridged the navigation gap between Peninsula Lake and Lake of Bays, hauling passengers on two ancient open-bench former electric streetcars. Passengers can now ride some of its equipment at the Muskoka Heritage Place. Leaving Huntsville, the tracks cross Lake Vernon and Hunters Bay. Between miles **166** and **172**, the train crosses the Magnetawan River four times. The South River is crossed first at mile **189**, and then at mile **194** Viaduct Creek is crossed on a 228-metre (750-foot) long trestle.

Route Highlights

North Bay to Englehart
Temagami Subdivision

Miles 1–138: Trout Lake can be seen to the east at mile **3**. The route then winds through a region of forests and lakes, with the tracks forming the eastern boundary of the Nipissing Forest Reserve. You continue to pass bodies of water, including Lake Temagami (mile **71**), and Rib Lake (miles **86** and **87**). At Cobalt, located near the famed mineral find that the railway profited from, the train passes the town located above, seen on the cliff to the west, and reaches the station at mile **102**. Lake Temiskaming (mile **107**) is seen to the east behind Haileybury. You then travel through a large agricultural region known as The Great Clay Belt. You get a good view of the area to the west, from miles **124** through **126**. You cross the Englehart River at mile **138** before reaching the modern station at the town by the same name. Here is a tribute to the line's rich history with locomotive 701 on display.

A plaque at the Gravenhurst station that tells of the area's rail heritage.

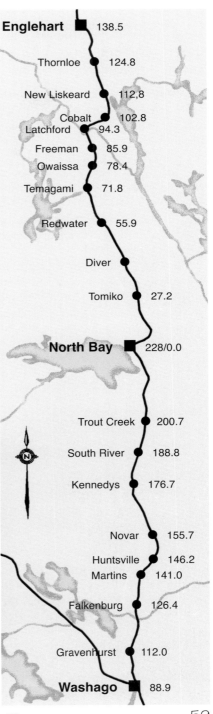

Englehart	138.5
Thornloe	124.8
New Liskeard	112,8
Cobalt	102.8
Latchford	94.3
Freeman	85.9
Owaissa	78.4
Temagami	71.8
Redwater	55.9
Diver	
Tomiko	27.2
North Bay	228/0.0
Trout Creek	200.7
South River	188.8
Kennedys	176.7
Novar	155.7
Huntsville	146.2
Martins	141.0
Falkenburg	126.4
Gravenhurst	112.0
Washago	88.9

Route Highlights

Englehart to Porquis
Ramore Subdivision

Miles 0–86: The train crosses the Blanche River at mile **7** before returning to the rocky outcroppings of the Canadian Shield. At Swastika (mile **26**), you pass through a park-like setting featuring a waterfall. A high trestle at mile **58** crosses the Little Wildgoose Creek. As you cross the trestle above the Driftwood River at mile **79**, look to the west to see the Montieth Correctional Facility. You reach Porquis at mile **86**, where you have a good opportunity to photograph the entire train as it travels around a curve.

The last 28 miles are travelled on the Devonshire Subdivision through an area with rolling hills, sandy soils, and tall fir trees. Mile **28** brings you to Cochrane, the final stop.

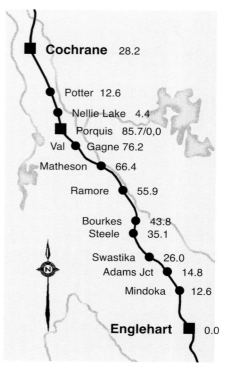

Cochrane 28.2
Potter 12.6
Nellie Lake 4.4
Porquis 85.7/0,0
Val Gagne 76.2
Matheson 66.4
Ramore 55.9
Bourkes 43.8
Steele 35.1
Swastika 26.0
Adams Jct 14.8
Mindoka 12.6
Englehart 0.0

The Cochrane Station Inn awaits travellers. — *Ontario Northland photo*

Polar Bear Express

The journey to the edge of the Arctic begins in Cochrane. Once the site of a First Nations meeting place along the overland pack trail to Moosonee, it was chosen by surveyors to be the junction of the *Temiskaming and Northern Ontario Railway* and the east-west *National Transcontinental Railway*. Incorporated in 1910, Cochrane continues to be a destination for the adventurous in all seasons. Located close to the station is the Cochrane Railway and Pioneer Museum. Headed up by *T&NO* steam locomotive No. 137, visitors board passenger cars and go back in time to learn about the region's history, and its local hometown hockey hero, Tim Horton.

Two trains connect from here to Moosonee. *The Little Bear* makes the trip throughout the year on a limited schedule, with a train comprising both freight and passenger cars. In the summer months, *The Polar Bear Express* is a popular tourist train that does a one day round-trip, every day except Mondays. For reservations call: 800-268-9281. Arriving by train, from any direction, we recommend the Cochrane Station Inn. Train and bus operations are on the main floor. There are 23 comfortable rooms on the second floor. You can make a reservation by calling 800-265-2356. E-mail: *stninn@onlink.net*. You can also contact the Cochrane Tourist Association, PO Box 2240, Cochrane, ON P0L 1C0. Call: 800-354-9948. Web: *www.puc.net/cochrane.htm*

Route Highlights

Cochrane to Moosonee
Island Falls Subdivision

Miles 0–186: Just beyond Cochrane, white daisies crowd the areas along the track. Watch for the white signs that announce the river names along with the elevation. The first is seen at mile **11** before you cross the Abitibi River. Gardiner Lake sits to the west at mile **18**. River crossings continue at East Jaw Bone Creek (mile **27**) and West Jawbone Creek (mile **29**). At mile **43** the communications tower to the east brings the outside world to Northern Ontario. Next, at mile **44**, the Abitibi River is crossed again. Between miles **56** and **67** the train travels through an area that was destroyed by forest fire in 1976. Highway 634 (crossed at mile **69**) is the last road you will see until Moosonee. The only way north now, other than the train, is by plane, canoe, or foot!

The tracks curve at mile **73**, giving you a good view to the east over the trees. The "Keep Out" signs at mile **80** mark where there was once a radar base. At this point you are also crossing the 50th parallel. From miles **84** to **89** you travel through another burnt-out area. Look to the east at mile **85** into the blackened trees for two old rusty boxcars, left from the 1975 Foxville train wreck. At mile **93**, to the east, you get a good look at the Otter Rapids power-generating station. The terrain begins to change as you enter the Hudson Bay lowlands.

Coral, at mile **96**, features a well-kept camp on the east side of the tracks. On the west side you can see the concrete foundations where the station and octagonal water tower once stood. The buildings of Moose River (mile **141.8**) remain today, but the old school house has been transformed into a railway bunkhouse. The Moose River is crossed on an impressive 548-metre (1,800-foot) long bridge. At mile **159** you cross the 51st parallel. A series of "upside-down" bridges, reversed so ice can pass underneath, are crossed. Between miles **174** and **180**, the train crosses three rivers, the Kwataboahegan (mile **174**), Hancock Creek (mile **176.5**), and Maidmans Creek (mile **180**). Finally, after crossing Store Creek, you arrive at Moosonee Station, mile **186**.

Started in 1903 when the Revillon Freres set up a trading post here, the community flourished with the coming of the railway in 1932. Visitors will enjoy visiting the displays in the railway baggage car, the Revillon staff house, and the numerous shops. Board the tour boat or the more traditional freighter canoes to cross the Arctic tidewaters on the Moose River to Moose Factory. This community dates back to 1673 as a Hudson's Bay Company outpost. After passing the modern hospital at the public docks, you can walk along Front Street, past the 1860 St. Thomas Anglican Church (which almost floated away during a 1912 flood—holes were drilled in the floor as a preventative measure) to the Moose Factory Centennial Museum. Here you can examine some of the island's original buildings, including the Hudson's Bay Company staff house, and a blacksmith shop built in 1740. You can also visit some teepees, where First Nations women prepare bannock, and children sell fossilized rocks, before returning to Moosonee and boarding your train to travel south.

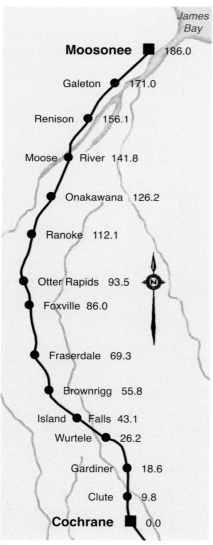

James Bay

Moosonee ■ 186.0

Galeton ● 171.0

Renison ● 156.1

Moose ● River 141.8

Onakawana 126.2

Ranoke 112.1

Otter Rapids 93.5

Foxville 86.0

Fraserdale 69.3

Brownrigg 55.8

Island ● Falls 43.1

Wurtele ● 26.2

Gardiner ● 18.6

Clute ● 9.8

Cochrane ■ 0.0

The Lake Superior

he story of Sudbury has long been associated with the region's minerals, most notably nickel. The popular tale of how *Canadian Pacific Railway* blacksmith Tom Flanagan discovered the nickel in the area is still told. When the *Canadian Pacific*'s transcontinental line was being built through the area, Flanagan threw a hammer towards an advancing fox. He missed and the hammer struck a rock, uncovering nickel and copper. Although he failed to see the value of the shiny rock, prospectors soon staked claims and the community grew. Today Sudbury is the largest nickel-producing area in the country.

The history of VIA Rail Canada's *Lake Superior* dates to 1955, when *Canadian Pacific* introduced *The Canadian* as trains 1 and 2. Then the *Imperial Limited* train, which made almost all scheduled stops, was renumbered to trains 17 and 18. When the *Imperial Limited* was discontinued and service was required for the area's residents who had rail-only access, the train was replaced by self-propelled Budd Rail Diesel Cars then operating between Sudbury and Thunder Bay as trains 417 and 418.

Today The Lake Superior trains are numbered 185 and 186, servicing isolated towns, fishing and hunting camps, and residences between Sudbury and White River. Despite the train's name, not once can you see Lake Superior during your trip through this Great Lakes forest region.

Although VIA's *Canadian* operates through Sudbury, it does not use the same station as *The Lake Superior*. The latter uses the *Canadian Pacific* station located in downtown Sudbury. A short walk up the hill from there is the Quality Inn, located at 390 Elgin Street South, Sudbury, ON P3B 1B1. You can even ask for a room facing the tracks! Reservations can be made at: 800-461-1120. Web: *www.qualityinn.sudbury.com*

As there is no meal service available on the train, we recommend you purchase something for lunch before departing. Sudbury is located at mile **79** of the Cartier Subdivision, where our trip begins.

Route Highlights

Sudbury to Cartier
Cartier Subdivision

Miles 79–113. On the station platform,

White River 129.9

O'Brien 120.2 Amyot 110.0 Girdwood 100.7 Swanson 88.8 Franz 82.0 Lochalsh 68.1 Missanabie 57.9 Carry 50.0 Dalton 44.2 Bolkow 35.1 Wayland 27.7 Musk 18.3 Esher 8.8 Chapleau Devon 136.4 130.1 Nemegos

before the train is boarded, you might see everything from a month's worth of groceries to a 17-foot aluminum boat and motor. As you leave the station, you can see the Sudbury Arena to the north. The city's most noticeable landmark, INCO's 381-metre (1,250-foot) high smokestack, can be clearly seen to the south at mile **80.** At mile **81,** the train crosses the INCO railway that services the mine. At mile **86** the train begins to pass through the agricultural area of the Blezard Valley. The tracks cross the Vermillion River at mile **97.** Then, at mile **101** the terrain becomes more rugged—to the north you can see the white water of the Onaping Falls. To the south between miles **103** and **105** is Windy Lake Provincial Park. Watch the sky near mile **110** at Crab Lake for cranes and owls native to the area. The train arrives at Cartier at mile **113.**

Route Highlights

Cartier to Chapleau
Nemegos Subdivision

Miles 0–136: After Cartier, the train becomes a lifeline to the remote communities along the tracks. The resourceful cottage owner at mile **11** on Stralak Lake uses a windmill of barrel halves to power a pump that brings water from the lake to the house. Between miles **13** and **30** the train travels through the scenic Spanish River Valley, crossing the river itself at mile **23.** With the Spanish on the north side of the tracks at mile **24.6,** look to the south to see the Little Pogamasing River. This cascading water comes from Lake Fluorite, located on the other side of the ridge. Mile **30.5** provides your last view of the Spanish River. You can't get much more isolated than the Bon Amis cabin at mile **32.9.** Metagama (mile **36**) is a popular starting place for hunters and trappers. The lake to the north at mile **51** features a cabin built by Albert Crolick, who worked this section of the railway for over forty years. The General Store at the small community of Biscotasing (mile **54**) can be seen behind the small station shelter, and you can also see the southernmost tip of Biscotasi Lake. Ramsey (mile **70**) is a loading area for the lumber industry. The A-frame building you can see was a church in the town's heyday; today it is a cottage.

The Lake Superior continues to traverse many water routes along the line: Bowen Creek (mile **77**), Woman River (mile **86**), and the Walkami River (mile **94**). In 1956, lumbering came to an end

The Lake Superior — Contact information on page 7

in Sultan (mile **96**), when the town's sawmill burnt down. Piles of sawdust at Kormak (mile **106**) are all that is left of this town that also once featured a large lumber mill. The train crosses the Nemegos River at mile **121**, and passes Poulin Lake on the south at mile **126**. The deteriorating wooden chutes at Devon (mile **130**) were once used to load boxcars with wood chips that would be processed into chipboard.

You arrive at Chapleau at mile **136**. On the north side sits the railway roundhouse with the modern station on the south side of the yards. This is a major station stop, so you will probably have time to stretch your legs behind the station at Chapleau's Centennial Park. Located here are former CPR steam locomotive 5433 and an historical plaque on French-Canadian author Louis Hemon. The log building houses the Chapleau Museum and Tourist Information Centre, featuring a taxidermy display of

local animals and railway memorabilia. If you are planning to visit the area for an extended period, we recommend you contact the Chapleau Regional Development Corporation, PO Box 1776, 34 Birch St., Chapleau, ON P0M 1K0. Call: 877-774-7727.

Web: *www.town ship.chapleau.on.ca*

Route Highlights
Chapleau to White River
White River Subdivision

Miles 0–129: Once you have left the Chapleau station, you proceed through the yards and cross the Chapleau River, which forms the eastern border of the Chapleau Crown Game Reserve. The line you are travelling on forms the southern border of the reserve; the western border is the *Algoma Central Railway*, and the northern border is the *Canadian National* mainline. Chapleau Crown is the world's biggest reserve with 700,000 hectares (200,000 acres) of wilderness setting. Watch the forest for bears, and the low swampy areas for moose, both of which are abundant in this area. Between miles **15** and **27** you can see the impressive Lake Windermere to the south. The lake was named by an English sportsman who was homesick; this large lake reminded him of his favorite fishing spot back home. Perhaps he also enjoyed fishing for the speckled trout in Sleith Lake to the south at mile **46**. At mile **55**, you first see Bay on Dog Lake; it was named before curves on the route were removed, and the line was shortened by two miles. Missanabie at mile **57** is one of the oldest communities in the area—it was once the site of a rest station along the overland pack trail to James Bay. People still come here for a rest at cottages

VIA Rail's *The Lake Superior* travels past Poulin Lake on a sunny fall day.

on the shores of Dog Lake, which we last see to the south at mile **66**. Mile **76** is a good spot to photograph moose in the swamp; if there are none, take a picture of your train on the curve. At mile **81** you can see miles to the south along narrow Hobon Lake; on the west shore you can see some of the few remaining buildings in Franz and the *Algoma Central Railway*, detailed on page 67. After passing through a small rock cut, you can see the concrete foundation of the former water tower. You then cross the tracks of the *Algoma Central Railway*. Look to the south at mile **88.3** as you cross the Magpie River to see a dam that regulates the water level on the long and narrow Esnagi Lake to the north. As you pass Summit Lake (mile **105**), the train has reached the highest point on the route of *The Lake Superior*.

Mile **107** is known as the Bermuda Triangle of the White River Subdivision for the odd occurrences here. In the 1940s the westbound train personnel reported a fire at the camp belonging to engineer Jack Hargass. They presumed he had fallen asleep with a burning cigarette. The following morning an RCMP officer was dispatched from White River to make a report. He found Mr. Hargass dead with a bullet wound in his head. Shortly afterwards two men where overheard boasting about how they had gotten away with the crime. Authorities were alerted and the two men were ar-

rested, with the victim's railway watch in their possession. After being identified by the jeweller in Chapleau this evidence was used to convict them.

In another eerie episode from the 1950s, Buddy Weedon came to close up his cabin for the fall, only to disappear mysteriously with only his empty wallet to be found. You will be glad to see the shores of Negwazu Lake at mile **110** and to be away from this troubled area.

The train crosses the White River twice at miles **122** and **127**. Rounding the curve and entering town of White River, you see a stately house on the hill that was built in 1903 for the *Canadian Pacific* superintendent. Today it houses the Creations Gallery. You arrive at the large brick station at mile **129**.

Originally called Snow Bank, the name changed with the arrival of the railway in 1885. A popular time to visit is during Winnie's Hometown Festival. This mid-August event celebrates the famous bear cub (later named Winnie the Pooh) that was purchased by Lieutenant Harry Colebourn on the station platform while travelling with his regiment enroute to England during WWI. You can learn more about the town at the White River Museum located on the corner of Elgin and Superior. After your long day on the rails, we recommend the Continental Motel, located on Highway 17. Reservations can be made at: 800-822-3616. Let them know if you are arriving by rail.

Algoma Central

The *Algoma Central Railway* was the vision of industrialist Francis H. Clergue, who began construction of the line in 1899 to bring iron ore from the north to the Algoma Steel Mill in Sault Ste. Marie. It was envisioned that the railway would one day terminate on the shores of Hudson Bay, but after construction reached Hearst in 1914, it went no further.

Today you can ride the Agawa Canyon Tour Train from June to mid-October, and the Snow Train on weekends, late December to mid-March. Or, you can travel to Hearst on the regularly scheduled passenger train year-round. Bring your snowmobile to ride the northern trails in the winter, or ride in elegance in the private car *Agawa*, which is available for charters.

Members of the famous Group of Seven painters once used a converted boxcar as their base from which to paint the region's incredible scenery. Now, with a few more creature comforts, you can spend a week in the Canyon View Camp Car and have the Agawa Canyon Park all to yourself when the sun sets. To learn more or to make a reservation, contact Algoma Central Railway Inc. Passenger Sales, PO Box 130, Sault Ste. Marie, ON P6A 6Y2. Call: 800-242-9287. Web: *www.algomacentralrailway.com*

Arriving or departing Sault Ste. Marie, we recommend the very convenient Quality Inn located directly across from the *Algoma Central* station at 180 Bay Street. Reservations can be made at: 800-228-5151 or visiting: *www.choicehotels.ca*

Algoma Central Railway tour excursion departs the Agawa Canyon Park.

Route Highlights

Sault Ste. Marie to Hawk Junction
Soo Subdivision

Miles 0–164: Departing the Soo, you pass a large paper mill and cross under the international bridge that connects to Sault Ste. Marie, Michigan; the tracks then curve to the north. To the west is the Algoma Steel complex and to the east are the railway shops. A turntable, used to turn locomotives, is located inside the square engine house to prevent the turntable pit from filling up with snow. At mile **3** look to the west for the view of the city, with St. Mary's River in the background. You pass over Highway 17 first at mile **7** and then at mile **14**. At mile **20** get your camera ready for the Bellevue Valley, which you cross on a 246-metre (810-foot) trestle. To the west at mile **27** sits the forested Goulais River Valley. You see the Searchmount ski trails to the east at mile **30**, before crossing the Goulais River at mile **31**. Over the next several miles, you pass a number of lakes and rivers: Achigan Lake on the east at mile **44**, Ogidaki Lake (mile **48**); the South Branch of the Chippewa River (mile **52**); Trout Lake (mile **62**), with large boulders that dot the water's surface; the North Branch of the Chippewa River (mile **69**); and Mongoose Lake at miles **74** and **75**. The Batchewana station is passed at mile **79** before the train crosses the river of the same name at mile **80**. As the train ascends through a forest, you get a great view over the Batchewana Valley to the east at mile **84** and Rand Lake at mile **86**.

Mile **92** brings you to the Montreal River Bridge. Built during the summer of 1902 by the Canadian Bridge Company, this 472-metre (1,550-foot) curved bridge

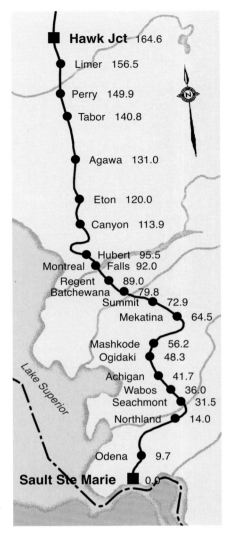

Hawk Jct 164.6
Limer 156.5
Perry 149.9
Tabor 140.8
Agawa 131.0
Eton 120.0
Canyon 113.9
Hubert 95.5
Montreal Falls 92.0
Regent 89.0
Batchewana 79.8
Summit 72.9
Mekatina 64.5
Mashkode 56.2
Ogidaki 48.3
Achigan 41.7
Wabos 36.0
Seachmont 31.5
Northland 14.0
Odena 9.7
Sault Ste Marie 0.0

features great views to both sides. Located directly below is a concrete dam that was poured around the fifteen steel girder footings. The dam supplies power to the region; the two cylindrical surge tanks for the dam can be seen to the west. After Frater at mile **102**, keep watching to the west to see the mighty Lake Superior and the twisting Trans-Canada Highway. You are now descending to the Agawa Canyon, with views continuing on the east

Algoma Central Railway — Contact information on page 67

The Scenic Agawa Canyon.

the line north of here was removed from the Perry Pit at mile **150**. At mile **152** the Michipicoten River is crossed. At Hawk Junction, a subdivision extends 26 miles to Lake Superior. If you have time, look inside the waiting room of the brick Hawk Junction Station, with its ornate ticket window. You can step back in time as you view the large promotional pictures of the region in its heyday.

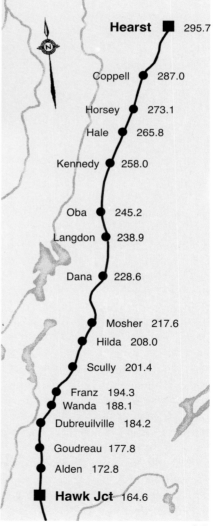

Hearst ▪ 295.7
Coppell ● 287.0
Horsey ● 273.1
Hale ● 265.8
Kennedy ● 258.0
Oba ● 245.2
Langdon ● 238.9
Dana ● 228.6
Mosher 217.6
Hilda 208.0
Scully 201.4
Franz 194.3
Wanda 188.1
Dubreuilville 184.2
Goudreau 177.8
Alden 172.8
Hawk Jct ▪ 164.6

side of the train. The Agawa River is crossed at mile **112** on a low bridge. Watch for Bridal Falls to the east and Black Beaver Falls to the west as you approach Agawa Canyon Park at mile **113**.

If you are on the tour train, you will find much to do here during your layover. Enjoy your picnic lunch, buy a reminder of your visit in the old railway passenger car souvenir shop car, hike one of the well-groomed trails, or climb the over-300 stairs to the canyon lookout for a view you will not soon forget. Railway enthusiasts will enjoy the *Algoma Central* memorabilia on display in the shelter near the track motorcars.

The canyon narrows past the park, leaving room for only the tracks and the river. Soon, the river widens and the train criss-crosses it three times: at miles **120**, **122**, and **130**. Until mile **138**, the railway line forms the eastern border of the Lake Superior Provincial Park. The ballast for

Route Highlights

Hawk Junction to Hearst
Northern Subdivision

Miles 165–296: After leaving Hawk Junction, the train returns to the forests of the Great Lakes Region. Goudreau (mile **177.8**) was once a gold mining town; you can still see the crumbling foundation and chimney from a smelter. Watch for Herman Lake to the east at mile **180**. At Dubreuilville (mile **184**) one of the largest lumber mill operations on the line can be seen to the west. Franz (mile **194.3**) was named after W.J. Franz, an early superintendent of Algoma Steel. This is also where you cross the *Canadian Pacific* east-west mainline, first seen to the east on the opposite shore of Hobon Lake. In the early years of the railway, this town was a thriving community. It turned into a ghost town, however, when fewer people were needed to operate the railways, and a controlled burn even removed a number of abandoned houses in 1980s. As you pass the CPR line, you might catch a glimpse of VIA Rail's *Lake Superior* train that operates on CPR track between Sudbury and White River (see page 63). While crossing the tracks, you can also see the concrete foundation still remaining from the former water tower to the east.

From here to Oba, the tracks form the western border of the Chapleau Game Reserve. St. Julien Lake (mile **198**) features a unique boulder-lined shore. Try to get your fellow passengers to spell Wabatongushi as you pass this large lake at mile **206**. Mile **207** brings you to the Arctic watershed; all the water to the south of here flows to Lake Superior and, north of here, to Hudson Bay. Oba Lake sits to the west at mile **209**. At mile **211** the train crosses a low bridge known as a floating bridge because the supports are sunk deep into the bottomless muskeg on the lake's floor. You can see the tops of the poles of the former bridge beside the modern bridge, which was installed in 1998. Another floating bridge is crossed at mile **214**. In the distance to the west, Tatnall Lodge can be seen on an island at mile **215.5**, before the train leaves Oba Lake at mile **216**. The Price Lodge at mile **221** was built with used telegraph poles from along the line.

The *Canadian National* mainline is crossed at Oba at mile **245**; this is the route of VIA Rail's *Canadian*. The population of this remote railway community has dwindled, but a number of buildings still remain. If you are changing trains here, Doreen's Handy Store is a good place to grab a snack, or some last minute items if you are starting a camping or canoe trip. At mile **247** the train crosses the Mattawitchewan River. Moose are sometimes spotted in the swamps along the route, so keep watching for these majestic animals. The terrain is quite flat as you arrive in Hearst at mile **295.7**.

After a long day's journey, we recommend the Companion Hotel (930 Front Street), only a few steps from where the train arrives and departs Hearst. Reservations can be made at: 888-468-9888.

VIA's Canadian

If you wanted to travel to western Canada in the 1870s, you had to travel by train through the northern United States, then north by riverboat to Winnipeg. The province of British Columbia joined Confederation based on Canada's promise that a railway would soon unite the new province to the remainder of the country. The country's first prime minister, John A. Macdonald, was one of many who envisioned a line of steel that would traverse the Canadian Shield in Ontario, the vast prairies, the unexplored mountains, and connect to the Pacific Ocean.

Before the country could come of age, it had the huge challenge of overcoming its own size and terrain. At the government's request, the *Canadian Pacific Railway* took on the challenge, overcame many

Places to enjoy a meal and meet fellow travellers onboard. *— Lloyd Smith photos*

obstacles, and connected east to west by rail. After the last spike was driven home on November 7, 1885, at Craigellachie BC, untouched land began to open at a rapid pace as the railway boom had reached the west. Soon other railways wanted a piece of the action, and challenged the CPR monopoly by racing to the Pacific. Competition was fierce between the various railways, and these others did not survive. The government was eventually forced to step in and combine them into *Canadian National Railways*. Even with two major players, competition for freight and passengers continued to be strong. If one did something, the other was always quick to follow. This was never more evident than in 1955, when the CPR introduced its newest transcontinental train *The Canadian*, and the CNR kept pace with the *Super Continental*.

Fortunately, there were enough passengers to go around and ridership remained high until the 1960s. Automobiles and airlines continued to win an ever-larger share of passenger traffic. As ridership declined, both railways wanted out of the rail passenger business.

In the late 1970s, Canada's government formed *VIA Rail Canada* to operate passenger trains on both CPR and CNR. VIA inherited outmoded railway equipment, using it until the 1980s. It then decided to rebuild the stainless steel fleet that the *Canadian Pacific* originally purchased in the 1950s. The renovations included replacing the steam heat with an electrical system, improving the air conditioning, replacing the outmoded electrical system, and adding showers. As the renewal progressed, the federal government instructed VIA to reorganize its transcontinental trains. In 1990, the daily *Canadian* and *Super Continental* services were rationalized. VIA provided a reduced frequency service connecting Toronto and Vancouver over the route of the former *Super Continental* and the *Canadian National* mainline. The name "*Canadian*" endured.

For beginning or finishing this cross-Canada journey, spend your time at Toronto's Fairmont Royal York Hotel. This classic railway hotel is located across the street from Union Station at 100 Front Street West. Reservations can be made at: 800-441-1414. Web: *www.fairmont.com*

Before you visit Toronto or anywhere in Ontario, we suggest you contact Ontario Travel Information Centre, Eaton Centre, Level 1, PO Box 104, 220 Yonge Street, Toronto, ON M5B 2H1. Call: 800-ONTARIO (668-2746). Web: *www.ontariotravel.net*

Route Highlights

Departing Toronto
Newmarket & York Subdivisions

Miles 0–13: VIA's Train No. 1 departs Toronto's Union Station in a westerly direction. Look to the south and straight up to see Toronto's most distinctive attraction, the CN Tower. Your train will then pass under the John Street pedestrian walkway connecting downtown Toronto with the CN Tower and Skydome. While passing under the bridge, notice the switch house that had to lose its roof for the walkway's construction. After passing Skydome, the tracks are below the city level. Above and to the south, you see a memorial dedicated to the Chinese railway workers who helped to construct the *Canadian Pacific Railway*. The train then turns north and travels on the Newmarket Subdivision until mile **13**. Here it will be turned on what is known as a wye, permitting the train to travel east on the York Subdivision, before reaching the Bala Subdivision at mile **16**. The train then turns northward.

Route Highlights

Arriving Toronto
Bala Subdivision

Mile 16–0: VIA's Train No. 2 into Toronto uses a different route from the one on which it departs. You'll arrive from the north on the eastern side of the city's core. You wind along the Don River Valley before connecting with the Kingston Subdivsion. The last two miles are spent navigating the trackage into Toronto's Union Station. Lake Ontario can be seen to the south. Before entering the station, to the north you can look down Toronto's famous Yonge Street. The restored Bank of Montreal building on the corner is the Hockey Hall of Fame, where the Stanley Cup is displayed. Then you reach the trainshed for Toronto's Union Station, located directly across from the Royal York Hotel.

CN Tower.

Union Station and the Royal York Hotel.

Canadian National Railway's steam locomotive 6077 today is on display in Capreol at the Northern Ontario RR Museum.

Route Highlights

Toronto to Capreol
Bala Subdivision

Mile 16–25: The Bala Subdivision is also used by many of Toronto's GO Transit trains, and you pass several GO commuter stations while travelling through the city's suburbs.

Miles **26–88**: North of the city the train travels through a forested region. Lake Simcoe can be seen to the west between miles **60** and **66**. The Talbot River, part of the Trent-Severn Canal/ Waterway, is crossed at mile **67**. At mile **71**, to the west, an old CPR station lives on as Box Car Willy's Restaurant. With Lake Couchiching to the west, the train arrives at Washago (mile **88**). This is where the *Northlander* continues on the Newmarket Subdivision (detailed on page 58). At Miles **89.8** and **100** you cross the Severn River, the most northerly river of the Trent-Severn Canal/Waterway.

Miles **101–145**: The *Canadian* travels through the scenic Muskoka cottage country. Three crossings, Coulter's Narrows (mile **112**), Jeanette's Narrows (**113**), and the Wallace Cut (**115**) are waterways that connect Bala Bay on the west to Lake Muskoka on the east.

Miles **146–151**: You pass through Parry Sound on a sharp curve. To the west you can see the 516-metre (1,695-foot) long CPR Seguin River trestle before arriving the Parry Sound station at mile **150**.

Miles **152–226**: The Canadian Shield becomes more predominant as the *Canadian* crosses many rivers flowing towards Georgian Bay. The Magnetawan River is crossed at mile **183.9**, then the Still River at mile **187.9**. A bridge high above the river at mile **193** offers a good view to both sides. The route follows Little Key River (miles **194–202**) before crossing the wide Key River at mile **203**. The train crosses the Pickerel River at miles **215** and **216**, then the French River at mile **218**. The Hartley Marina can be seen below on the west side of the bridge. The shores of the river make up the French River Provincial Park, which is over 97-kilometres (60-miles) long and connects Georgian Bay to Lake Nipissing.

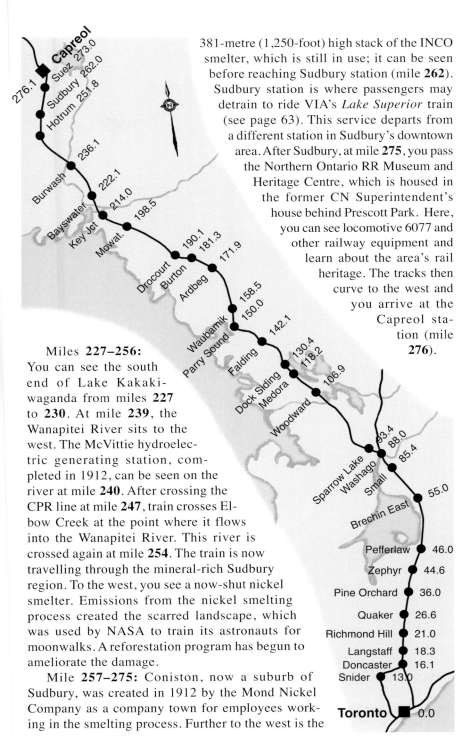

381-metre (1,250-foot) high stack of the INCO smelter, which is still in use; it can be seen before reaching Sudbury station (mile **262**). Sudbury station is where passengers may detrain to ride VIA's *Lake Superior* train (see page 63). This service departs from a different station in Sudbury's downtown area. After Sudbury, at mile **275**, you pass the Northern Ontario RR Museum and Heritage Centre, which is housed in the former CN Superintendent's house behind Prescott Park. Here, you can see locomotive 6077 and other railway equipment and learn about the area's rail heritage. The tracks then curve to the west and you arrive at the Capreol station (mile **276**).

Miles 227–256: You can see the south end of Lake Kakakiwaganda from miles **227** to **230**. At mile **239**, the Wanapitei River sits to the west. The McVittie hydroelectric generating station, completed in 1912, can be seen on the river at mile **240**. After crossing the CPR line at mile **247**, train crosses Elbow Creek at the point where it flows into the Wanapitei River. This river is crossed again at mile **254**. The train is now travelling through the mineral-rich Sudbury region. To the west, you see a now-shut nickel smelter. Emissions from the nickel smelting process created the scarred landscape, which was used by NASA to train its astronauts for moonwalks. A reforestation program has begun to ameliorate the damage.

Mile **257–275:** Coniston, now a suburb of Sudbury, was created in 1912 by the Mond Nickel Company as a company town for employees working in the smelting process. Further to the west is the

VIA's Canadian — Contact information on page 7

Route Highlights

Capreol to Hornepayne
Ruel Subdivision

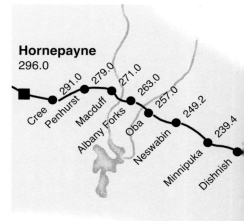

Hornepayne
296.0

Miles 0–2: There was a time when the Toronto and Montreal sections of the *Super Continental* were divided at Capreol to carry on east to each city or were consolidated into a single train travelling westbound. (A similar operation was performed in Sudbury to the south on the CPR's *Canadian*.) When originally built, the railway was directly south of Capreol. You can see the original route's bridge supports in the Vermillion River. Shortly after the line was built, however, Capreol was chosen as the site where the tracks from Montreal (now removed) would connect with the line to the west. At mile **1** you return to the original route on a tight curve. The river then widens to become Bass Lake.

Miles **2–18:** You can see first-hand the rugged terrain of the Canadian Shield, with its massive outcroppings of rocks and countless lakes that challenged the railway builders. Fraser Lake can be seen to the north at mile **9**. The rails continue to follow the Vermillion River, crossing it at again at mile **9.4** and **16.3**.

Mile **19**: In 1926 the Ontario Department of Education, the *Ontario Northland Railway*, the CPR, and CNR formed a unique partnership, creating six school cars. The cars featured a small living area for a teacher, family, and a classroom complete with chalkboard and a small library. The cars would be pulled behind a freight train and left in isolated

The train winds around the lakes and rock outcroppings of the Canadian Shield in northern Ontario.

76

communities for a week, to assist in teaching the children of railway and lumber workers, as well as woodsmen and First Nations children. Before leaving, the teacher would assign enough homework to keep the children busy until the car returned. The cars operated on the ONR from North Bay to Rib Lake; on the CPR from Chapleau to Cartier, and Cartier to White River; and three on the camps. Miles **63** to **65** take you past the shores of Kashnebawning Lake to the south at Westree. To the north at mile **76**, the lone trailer with its welcoming gate would make an interesting place to visit... but what would you do there? The Muskegogama River is crossed at mile **78**. Before reaching Gogama, at mile **86**, the train crosses Minnisinaqua Lake.

Miles **90–147**: On the curved causeway that crosses Windegoguinzing Lake at mile **90**, you get a good opportunity to photograph your train. The fishing must be good at mile **95**, because the lodge is called "Camp Brag-A-Lot." The former two-storey section-men's house at Stackpool (mile **105**) can be seen to the south a short distance from the tracks. At mile **134** a 345-metre (1,134-foot) long bridge crosses the Groundhog River. The train crosses the Muskego River at mile **145**.

CNR:
from Capreol to Foleyet, Port Arthur (Thunder Bay) to Fort Francis, and Sioux Lookout to the Manitoba border. Fred Sloman, who created the idea, worked on the Capreol to Foleyet car that featured stops at Raphoe (mile **19**), as well as Laforest, Ruel, Ostrom, Bethnal, and Stackpool. Today his car is preserved at Clinton, Ontario.

Miles **20–35**: The scenic lakes continue: Graveyard Lake (miles **27–30**); Post Lake (miles **30–31**); and Pine Lake and Smoky Lake (miles **32–35**).

Miles **36–89**: After crossing the Wahnipitae River at mile **45** you arrive at Felix (mile **46.8**) with its summer

Map labels:

jolis 213.6
205.9
194.8
186.4
183.2
Dunrankin
Agate
Elsas
176.5
Oatland
166.9
Missonga
158.0
Shawmere
148.3
Foleyet
141.4
Singe Lake
133.2
Kukatush
125.8
Tionag
Gladwick
115.6
105.4
Stackpool
95.5
Bethnal
86.6
Gogama
76.9
Makwa
68.6
64.3
Ostrom
Westree
59.3
Stupart
51.6
Ruel
39.9
Thorlake
30.0
Laforest
19.5
Raphoe
8.9
Milne
0.0
Capreol
N

Passing scenery is enjoyed from wraparound windows of the dome car.

Miles **148–183:** The railway created towns when steam locomotives had to be re-supplied with coal, water, and sand. The large concrete coaling tower still remains in Foleyet at mile **148**. At mile **179** the *Canadian* crosses the Nemegosenda River, and then the Kapuskasing River at mile **183**. The train then skirts the lake of the same name to the south before reaching Elsas, where an old CN caboose on the hill lives on as a camp. The river is the eastern border of the Chapleau Crown Game Reserve, the world's largest reserve, with 700,000 hectares (200,000 acres) of wilderness setting. The Reserve's other three borders are also formed by railway lines: the northern border is the line you are travelling on, while the western border is the *Algoma Central Railway*, and the southern border is the *Canadian Pacific Railway* mainline.

Miles **184–255:** At mile **194** the train passes four simple white crosses to the south. These mark a tragic accident that occurred in 1964 when a freight train ran into a passenger train, killing four CN employees. Another coaling facility stands alone at Fire River, mile **223**.

Miles **256–294:** The tracks cross those of the *Algoma Central Railway* at mile **257**. The ACR passenger train that operates between Sault Ste. Marie to the south and Hearst to the north is detailed on page 67. If you are changing trains in Oba, Doreen's Handy Store is a good place to grab a snack or last-minute items, especially if you are starting a camping or canoe trip. The area here is known for its fox, moose, and bears. If you see one, call out so everyone can get a look.

Arriving in Hornepayne, you pass the Hallmark Hornepayne Centre on the south side of the tracks. Completed in 1980, the 160,000-square foot town complex includes the town high school, a hotel, regional offices, library, apartments, a mall with stores and restaurants, the town swimming pool, medical centre, and rooms for railway crews to layover.

Route Highlights

Hornepayne to Armstrong
Caramat Subdivision

Miles 0–2: Hornepayne is a modern day refueling centre for railway locomotives, so there will be an extended stop here. The railway engine house to the north was built in 1921 and features an enclosed turntable used for switching locomotives onto different shop tracks. The turntable is enclosed because the large amounts of snow that fall here would fill the pit in which the turntable operates. This and another similar building used by the *Algoma Central Railway* in Sault Ste Marie are the last two active facilities of their kind in North America. The train then passes the unused two-storey Hornepayne brick station that was also built in 1921.

Miles **3–44:** *The Canadian* quickly returns to the northern wilderness. River crossings and lakes continue, with the Obakamiga River at mile **15**, the Stonet River at mile **27**, the Little Stoney River at mile **29**, and Flanders Lake at mile **30** to the south.

Watch the passing forest for the unique shape of the numerous spruce trees. The growth spurt on the top of these trees occurs during the short growing season each year. During the winter months, the lower portion of the tree remains dormant because of the extreme northern climate. This area is also the border between the Northeastern and Northwestern Ontario regions. Hillsport (mile **42**) is noted for its fishing lodges.

Mile **45–98:** In 1896 railway contractors Donald Mann and William Mackenzie purchased the charter to the build the *Lake Manitoba Railway and Canal Company*. In 1899 it merged with the *Winnipeg and Hudson Bay Railway* to form the *Canadian Northern Railway*. From this humble beginning in the Province of Manitoba, the two men created the country's second transcontinental railway. At mile **45.6** you cross the White Otter River where, on January 1, 1914, a cold ten-minute ceremony took place with company president William Mackenzie driving home the last spike on the *Canadian Northern Railway*. The tracks cross Bowler Lake at mile **66** and Little Charon Lake at mile **71**. At mile **78** Caramat Lake can be seen to the south.

Miles **99–130:** After passing through the lumber town of Longlac, with its modern station, *The Canadian* crosses Long Lake between miles **99** and **101**. This lake is 73 kilometres (45 miles) in length and 3.2 kilometres (2 miles) across. It was a major canoe route for "the voyageurs" between Hudson Bay and Lake Superior during the fur trade heyday. The large white church to the west makes a nice photograph. At Longlac Junction (mile **101**), the *Canadian Northern* turned south to Thunder Bay before carrying on to the west. Today, the *Canadian* travels north on a stretch of track built in 1923 and 1924 to connect the former *Canadian Northern* with the former *National Transcontinental Railway* mainline. The Kenogamissis River is crossed at mile **107** and Manitounamaig Lake can be seen to the north between miles **111** and **114**. As the train approaches Nakina, the tracks form the eastern border of the Moraine Provincial Nature Reserve.

Mile **131:** Before the Longlac-Nakina Cutoff opened on January 24, 1924, the section town of Grant had been located 17 miles to the east. With the decision to connect the two railways, the entire town of Grant was moved to the present site, and renamed Nakina. The two-storey Nakina Station, built around the same time, has been preserved by the community.

The train now rides on the line built by the *National Transcontinental Railway*. This line was formed in 1903 by legislation creating a unique partnership between the *Grand Trunk Railway* and the Federal Government under the leadership of Prime Minister Sir Wilfred Laurier. The newly formed *Grand Trunk Pacific Railway* was to build the portion west of Winnipeg, while the Government was to build the *National Transcontinental Railway* section to the east. To appease his own cabinet members, Laurier decided to build the NTR from Moncton, New Brunswick, through Quebec City, then on a route that travelled in an almost straight line through northern Quebec and Ontario to Winnipeg. It was agreed that the GTP would lease the line from the government and would be responsible for operating trains once the line was completed. In 1913, a passenger train travelled from Winnipeg to Quebec City over the new direct route.

In 1915, however, financial difficulties with its western lines forced the *Grand Trunk* to renege on its end of the deal to build the western portion of the rail line. The line came under the control of the *Canadian Government Railway*. It was later named *Canadian National Railways*, which inherited the transcontinental lines from both the NTR and *Canadian Northern*. The track east of Nakina to Calstock was abandoned in 1986 because of a lack of freight traffic. In 1991, the portion from Calstock to Cochrane was sold to the *Ontario Northland Railway*. A section of the line in Northern Quebec, between Hervey Junction and Senneterre, is the only other portion of the NTR between here and Quebec City where a passenger train is operated. VIA Rail's *Abitibi* is detailed on page 33.

Miles **132–197:** At mile **134**, the train passes Balkam Lake, followed by Exton Lake at mile **139**. You see Kawashkagama Lake to the south at mile **140**. The train crosses the Kawashkagama River (mile **147**) on a 68-metre (225-foot) long bridge. Creek and river crossings in the

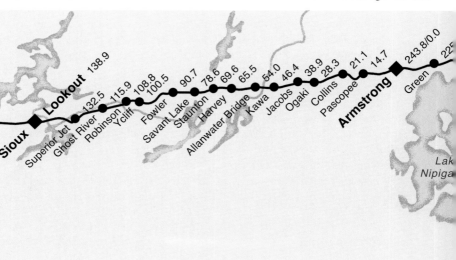

wilderness continue: Trout Creek (mile **148**), Johnson Creek (mile **153**), Emilie Creek (mile **176**), Spruce Creek (mile **180**), and the Ombabika River (mile **187**). Look to the north to see the large hydroelectric dam on Clod Lake. Minataree Lake can be seen to the north at mile **197**.

Miles **197–243**: One of the most impressive highlights of the Caramat Subdivision is the crossing of the 243-metre (798-foot) long Jackfish Creek Viaduct. The fast moving water of Jackfish Creek, 23 metres (75 feet) below, appears to cut straight through the solid rock of the Canadian Shield. Look over the trees to the south while on the bridge to see Ombabika Bay on Lake Nipigon. The most prominent building in Ferland is the yellow St. Joseph's Church at mile **213**. The 110-metre (362-foot) high Mud River Viaduct crosses 18 metres (59 feet) above this narrow river at mile **219**. The rustic community of the same name features a few log cabins. For the next 23 miles the tracks form the northern border of the Windigo Bay Provincial

Nature reserve, which extends to the shores of Lake Nipigon. Rapid Creek is crossed at mile **228**. Lakes to the north of the track include Jojo Lake at mile **235**, Flat Lake at mile **240**, and Red Granite Lake at mile **241**.

Communities that have been created to service the railway have long been named after the railway's financiers, employees, or even the construction foreman's children. Armstrong (mile **243**) was named after the NTR's Chief Engineer, T.S. Armstrong.

Armstrong has always been the dividing point for the CNR's eastern and western divisions. In the heyday of steam locomotives, those arriving from each district would be turned and sent back, pulling the next train. Today's diesels are not returned to their home base, but crews still change here, laying over at the large CN bunkhouse on the north side of the tracks. It features a screened-in summer porch, where employees can await their next departure without dealing with Northwestern Ontario mosquitoes.

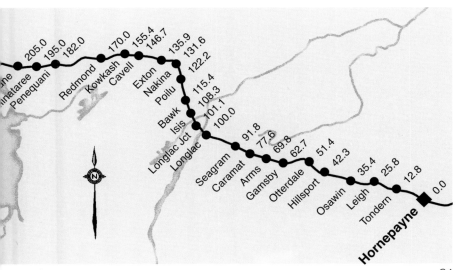

Route Highlights

Armstrong to Sioux Lookout
Allanwater Subdivision

Miles 0–2: In the 1950s, Armstrong had a Distant Early Warning (DEW) radar station north of town, manned by the US Air Force. Leaving town, you cross Highway 527, which connects Armstrong with Thunder Bay. Numerous lakes and river crossings continue along the route. The First Nations reserve at Collins can be seen to the south at mile **21**.

Mile **24–44:** The *Canadian* enters the Wabakimi Provincial Park. The train travels through the southern portion of this 892,000-hectare (2,204,000 acres) park. Keep your camera ready at mile **31** to get a photograph of the long narrow lake, located in a gorge, that parallels the tracks. Lakes and sweeping vistas continue over the next couple of miles. Since you cross the line between the Eastern and Central Time zones in this area, your travel clocks and watches should be moved one hour back if travelling west, or advanced one hour if travelling east. At mile **44**, a trail leads from here to a remote northern destination with the fitting name of Camp 44. The camp takes its name from the mileage on the subdivision where all the supplies are unloaded to begin the hike.

Miles **45–65:** At mile **53** the train crosses the northern tip of Kawaweogama Lake and arrives at the community of Allanwater Bridge (mile **54**). This community, which is only

Flint Landing fishing camp, on Heathcoate Lake, is accessible only by floatplane or a pedestrian bridge connecting to the railway tracks.

accessible by rail or by air, is a favourite destination for fishermen and canoeists. In the summer months it is quite common to see floatplanes tied up to the docks on the lake. You can also see the St. Barnabas United Church.

Miles **66–67:** Watch to the north for a unique wilderness setting, where a walk bridge (the only way across) connects the cottages on the island in Heathcote Lake to the mainland near the tracks. At mile **67** the train departs the Wabakimi Provincial Park.

Miles **75–76:** As you cross the road at mile **75** you can see the railway communication lines have been raised to allow the logging trucks to pass underneath.

Miles **78.6:** Savant Lake, on the hill beside the tracks to the north, was originally known as Buck Station after an NTR locomotive engineer. The name was changed when it was being confused with another town of the same name. In the 1940s, a local resident started the construction of a building featuring concrete walls with reinforced steel. He would not tell anyone what it was to be used for when it was completed. Before he could finish it, the man died, and the structure was never completed. The train then passes the Four Winds Motel.

Miles **78–106:** Between miles **91** and **99** the train snakes around numerous lakes and rock cuts. Listen at mile **100.8** to hear the wheels sing. If travelling at track speed, you can hear the sound of the wheels bouncing off the rocks while in the tight curve.

Miles **107–120:** The train crosses a bay on Marchington Lake (mile **107**), which can be seen to the north. Although the name Ghost River at mile **115.9** conjures up one's imagination, in fact it is a quiet community with a few houses and summer residences. Look to the north at mile **120** to see some rapids on the Sturgeon River, as well as the remains of an old mill on McDougall Bay.

Miles **121–132:** Bears and moose are numerous in the dense forest here, so watch the woods. The area at mile **132.9** here was once known as Superior Junction, because the Graham Subdivision split off the mainline towards Thunder Bay, before being removed in 1995-96. A mixed train service, which survived into the 1980s, featured a combination baggage-mail-and-passenger car attached to the rear of a freight train. The coach, built in the 1920s, provided rail passenger service to the isolated communities along the route. An example of this style of railway car is preserved at the Winnipeg Railway Museum.

Miles **133–139:** A 142-metre (465-foot) long bridge, with three steel spans, each 47-metres (155-feet) long, allows the *Canadian* to cross the Sturgeon River. At mile **137** the train passes under the modern highway to Thunder Bay before reaching the unique British-style Tudor station at Sioux Lookout. The town derives its name from the Ojibway First Nation people's use of the area's highest elevations to watch to the south for invading groups from the competing Sioux First Nation.

Route Highlights

Sioux Lookout to Winnipeg
Reddit Subdivision

Miles 0–11: Centennial Park separates the tracks and Sioux Lookout's Front Street on the ridge to the north. The town's First Nations heritage is reflected on the sign for the park, which is written in English and Ojicree (a combination of Cree and Ojibway languages). Leaving town, you can see Pelican Lake to the south before the train crosses it on a low 83-metre (272-foot) long bridge at mile **1.3**. Pelican Lake then continues on the north side of the train. The tracks cross two creeks at mile **4**: Marsh Creek at mile **4.4**, then Vermilion Creek at mile **4.5**.

Miles 12–16: The train follows Lost Lake for the next five miles. The community of Hudson (mile **12**) has long been a jump-off point for float planes that travel north. Today you can rent a houseboat and spend a week or more on Lost Lake. At mile **13**, the train passes a large lumber mill to the north.

Miles 17–41: The train travels through a large rock cut at mile **28**. At mile **31** Spine Lake can be seen to the north. The *Canadian* passes through a 99-metre (325-foot) long tunnel at mile **41**.

Miles 42–72: The northern view over Sunday Lake (mile **45**) makes for a nice photograph. The train then winds its way through the rock cuts. Instead of realigning Niddrie siding, which begins at mile **57**, the passing track actually goes around a railway signal light. The lake to the north here is Norse Lake; Walsh Lake is to the south. A wide rock cut had to be created at mile **65.5** where Morgan siding connects with the main track. Red Lake Road is passed at mile **71**.

A 53-metre (174-foot) long bridge crosses 17-metres (55-feet) above the Wabigoon River at mile **73**. While crossing the bridge, look directly below on the north side of the track to see a waterfall.

Miles 74–81: Near the village of Quibell, the Canadian Shield disappears briefly and the landscape changes to one of fields and pastures.

Miles 82–96: Get your camera ready as the train passes Canyon Lake, first seen on the north side of the tracks at mile **82.5**. The train passes through two separate tunnels, at miles **88** and **89**, each just over 150-metres (500-feet) long. There are more good views to the northwest at mile **92**. You get your last views of Canyon Lake at mile **95**. At mile **96** the train passes the creek that connects the lakes along the route.

Miles 97–105: Favel Lake is to the north between miles **97** and **103**. Between miles **106** and **108** the train passes Wild Lake.

Mile 113: The small Farlane Station sits quietly on the south side of the tracks. This was one of many stops made by the *Campers Special*, a unique train that served the area's cottagers. Lasting from 1911 to 1989, the idea was originally promoted by the CNR to secure more passengers, thus justifying more trains. The railway encouraged employees and other Winnipeggers to build cottages along the route; of course, the only way in or out was by train. Packed with bags, pets, and all the essentials needed by cottagers for a weekend getaway, the train would leave Winnipeg on Friday evenings, with passengers disembarking at the lakes along the way. It would remain in Sioux Lookout over the weekend and return to Winnipeg on Sunday, bringing home the weary weekenders.

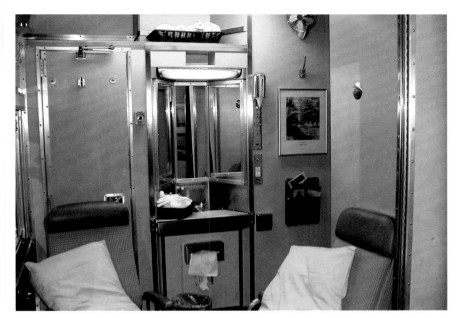

Daytime setup of a bedroom showing the vanity and entrance to the private bathroom.

Miles **114–122:** After passing through more rock cuts, keep watching to the north at mile **116**. Years of water running down the sheer cliff on the opposite side of the lake created some interesting streaks on the rock face. Also to the north at mile **117.5**, you can notice how the rocks on the far side of Seel Creek have given way and broken up on the shoreline. This was caused by water entering cracks in the rocks, expanding in freezing temperatures, eventually causing the rock to weaken and finally give way.

Mile **123:** As you arrive in Redditt, look to the hill to the north to see a Quonset-hut-style of building housing this small town's Canadian Legion Hall, and a former CNR steel caboose 79312 that contains a small museum. In its day Redditt was a large division point for the NTR and CNR. The site of the former railway yard is now a grass airstrip. A small portion of the roundhouse can still be seen in front of the large and picturesque Eagle Rock.

Miles **124–135:** The train runs beside the long and narrow Corn Lake, seen to the north from miles **124** to **126**. Then, at miles **130.4** and **135.3**, The *Canadian* travels through the last two tunnels before the Rocky Mountains.

Miles **136–137:** The train crosses the Winnipeg River at mile **136**. Look to both sides for good views while crossing the river. To the north was once the site of the grand Minaki Lodge that was built in 1927 and burned down in 2003. On the other side of the river you will arrive at the Minaki station, now home to the Blue Heron gift shop. Minaki is a First Nations word that translates into "Beautiful Country," which is quite fitting for the area.

Miles **138–144:** A public launch for putting boats into Gunn Lake can be seen to the north at mile **138**. At mile **139** to the north you get a good view over Pistol Lake. At mile **140** you cross Highway 596.

Miles **145–146:** The old right-of-way viewed to the north was changed because, on the east side of the rock cut, the original road bed was located in a swampy area that was impossible to stabilize. The railway later decided to move the tracks to more stable ground.

Miles **147–151:** A cabin, known as "the Haze," is tucked into the forest on the north side of the tracks at mile **150**. Watch for the name spelled out with white rocks on the front lawn. Then, you pass the station shelter at Ottermere, located on the south side.

Miles **152–154:** Malachi Lake, the most popular of cottage destinations, can be seen as the tracks round the northern end of the lake. The picturesque station, with the lake in the background, still remains at mile **153**.

Miles **155–162:** Mile **158** brings you through a rock cut featuring jagged sides. At White (mile **159**), a large rock quarry can be seen to the south. At Rice Lake (mile **160**) there is another station shelter to the south. Watch for the sign at mile **162**, announcing the Ontario/Manitoba border. Travelling west, you are also entering the Whiteshell Provincial Park.

Miles **163–178:** At mile **167** the white stuccoed building on the north side of the tracks, now a summer cottage, dates to 1927 as a section foreman's house. At mile **168** you travel high above narrow Cross Lake. When the railway was built, large amounts of fill were needed to carry the tracks over the lake's swampy bottom. Since the lake is part of the Whiteshell River system, it was necessary to blast through the rock so the water could continue to flow. It is a popular canoe route; when the water level is high, canoeists must climb the banks and portage over the tracks.

Miles **179–183:** After passing the stop for Brereton Lake (mile **179**), the lake can be seen to the north at mile **180**. This is also where the *Canadian* passes

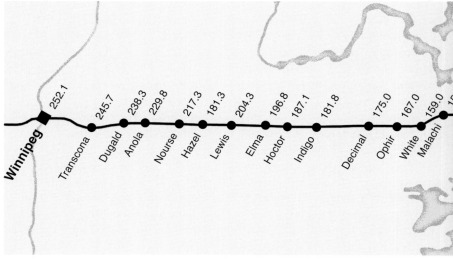

VIA's Canadian — Contact information on page 7

over the Rennie River, a popular snowmobile trail in the winter months. "Railfanning," is what railway enthusiasts call spending time waiting for trains to get that perfect photo. A favourite place in the area for the editor of *Canadian Railway Modeller* magazine to "railfan" is at mile **183.3**, where the *Canadian National* tracks cross high above the mainline of the *Canadian Pacific*.

Miles **184–190:** As the *Canadian* exits the Whiteshell Provincial Park, the Canadian Shield starts to disappear and the terrain gradually changes to a prairie landscape.

Miles **191–200:** The Whiteshell Provincial Forest is entered at mile **192**. At mile **196** the train crosses the Whitemouth River. To the north you can clearly see the dome of the Ruthenian Greek Catholic Parish of the Holy Cross. Elma is reminiscent of a prairie town of years gone by. The buildings along the highway include the old pool hall and confectionery and the Elma Hotel.

Miles **201–237:** At mile **201**, you leave the Whiteshell Provincial Forest and enter the Agassiz Provincial Forest. The train crosses the Brokenhead River at mile **211**. Watch for deer in the fields along the tracks. On the north side of the tracks at mile **229.8** you get a glimpse of the pioneer village of the Anola and District Museum, featuring a pioneer home, a one-room schoolhouse, and the area's first fire truck. At mile **236** the tracks cross highway 15 diagonally.

Mile **238:** Note the station sign while passing Dugald. This is the site of Manitoba's worst railway accident. It occurred here on September 1, 1947, as cottagers were returning to Winnipeg on the *Campers Special* after the long weekend. The train slammed into the eastbound *Continental*, killing thirty-one passengers and crew, and injuring eighty-five.

Miles **239–244:** The Winnipeg skyline to the west comes into view. At mile **243**, the train crosses the Winnipeg Floodway over a 275-metre (900-foot) long bridge. The City of Winnipeg is in the Red River Valley and recorded floods in the area date back to the early 1800s. After the

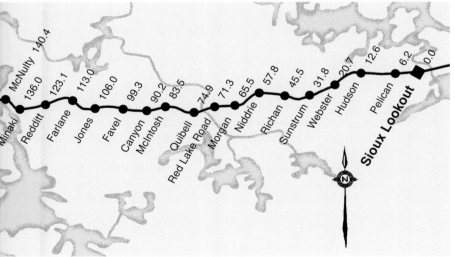

devastating flood of 1950, officials decided to build this large diversion so excess springtime flood waters from the Red River could bypass Winnipeg, and be returned to the normal river channel north of the city. Construction began in 1962 and it was put into service in 1969. It has since saved the city from flooding numerous times.

Miles **245–246**: The train passes CN's Transcona Shops. The name of this Winnipeg suburb, Transcona, is an abbreviation of "Transcontinental," derived from the name of the first railway through this area: *National Transcontinental Railway*.

Miles **247–252**: The train passes through an industrial area and, at mile **250**, crosses high above the CPR Emerson Subdivision. This was the first track on the Canadian Prairies built with the locomotive *Countess of Dufferin*, which arrived in Winnipeg in 1877 on a barge pushed by the stern-wheeler *Selkirk*. At mile **250.5** you cross the Seine River in the suburb of St. Boniface, which has the largest population of French-speaking Canadians in western Canada. To the north sits Whittier Park. The park, with its replica fort, is home to the Festival du Voyageur every February. To the south you see the silver roof of the College de St. Boniface. The *Canadian* crosses the mighty Red River at mile **251**. Once across, to the south is the Can West Global Park, home of the Winnipeg Goldeyes. The facade of the St. Boniface Basilica, with its round empty window, can be seen on the opposite side of the river. This is all that is left of the original Basilica, which burned down in 1968. A modern church was erected behind it. To the north you can look down Portage Avenue East to see what is referred to as "the Windiest corner in North America" — Portage and Main, the centre of the city's business district.

Finally, you arrive at Winnipeg's Union Station, designed by the same architects who worked on New York's Grand Central Station. Built for the *Grand Trunk Pacific* and the *Canadian Northern Railways*, it opened in 1911.

Winnipeg is derived from a Cree word that translates into "Muddy Waters," a reference to the silt from the region's fine soil that fills the Red and Assiniboine Rivers. The area was a First Nations settlement for years before the first Europeans, La Verendrye and a group of hearty explorers, first visited the encampment. Winnipeg was founded in 1738.

Before the railway came to Winnipeg, riverboats provided the major transportation link between the city and North Dakota. The railway changed all this, starting in 1878 when a rail link was built to Emerson on the Canada/US border. Soon rival companies were building a network of rail lines across the prairie. Before long, three lines headed for the Pacific Ocean, all of which had numerous subdivisions spread across the prairies to collect the region's plentiful harvests. West of Winnipeg, the *Canadian* travels on the line built by the *Grand Trunk Pacific*, which later became part of *Canadian National Railways*.

Winnipeg is the midway point for your journey. There is a scheduled one-hour stop for servicing and a change of crews. This gives you an opportunity to stretch your legs and see the opulent rotunda of the station. Also located in the station trainshed is the Winnipeg Railway Museum. Group tours are welcome

88

during the layover, but tours must be pre-arranged by calling: 204-942-4632.

Winnipeg is a great place to break your journey. Attractions include The Forks National Historic Site that is directly behind Union Station, and the Exchange District, featuring the renowned Museum of Man and Nature. Also in the area is UN Luggage at 175 McDermot Avenue, if you need to repair your luggage or purchase more to carry all your souvenirs.

For rail travellers to and from Winnipeg, the Hotel Fort Garry is very convenient. Built by the *Grand Trunk Pacific*, it is located directly across the street from the station at 222 Broadway Avenue. Reservations can be made at: 800-665-8088. Web: *www.fortgarryhotel.com*

For more travel information about the city of Winnipeg, contact Destination Winnipeg at 259 Portage Avenue, Winnipeg, MB R3B 2A9. Call: 800-665-0204.

Web: *www.tourism. winnipeg .mb.ca*

Winnipeg is also the starting point of VIA's *Hudson Bay* train to Churchill, which travels north from Portage La Prairie, Manitoba.

If you are continuing on to southern Manitoba, we recommend the Stationhouse B&B in Kleefeld, Manitoba, where visitors stay at the restored CPR station originally from Dominion City. Reservations can be made at: 204-377-4790. E-mail: *stationhouse@bigfoot.com*

If you are planning to explore Manitoba as part of your journey, we recommend that you visit the Travel Manitoba Centre in the Johnston Terminal at The Forks, or contact them at Travel Manitoba, 7th Floor, 155 Carlton Street, Winnipeg, MB R3C 3H8. Call: 800-665-0040. Web: *www.travelmanitoba.com*

The eastbound *Canadian* passes through the centre of the friendly city of Winnipeg, which is the train's mid-way point of the journey.

Route Highlights

Winnipeg to Melville
Rivers Subdivision

Miles 0–10: As you depart Winnipeg, you see buildings to the south that were once used by the *Northern Pacific Railway* (later CNR) and now comprise the Forks Market that features fresh produce, restaurants, and numerous curio shops. To the north is the green copper roof of the Hotel Fort Garry. As you cross the Assiniboine River (mile **0.2**), you see the junction of the Assiniboine and Red rivers below the former railway (now a pedestrian) bridge. To the north is the Main Street Bridge of the Old Forts.

The train curves to the west, high above the city's wide Main Street. Look to the north towards the downtown area, or to the south to see the Norwood Bridge. At mile **1** look north to see the distinctive green dome of the Manitoba Legislative Building. On the roof is the five-tonne statue of the Golden Boy, holding a sheaf of wheat in one hand and a light in the other to guide the way to prosperity. The statue was sculpted and plated with gold in Paris, France. It was on its way to Manitoba when World War One intervened. The ship carrying him served as a troop carrier, and he did not arrive until 1919. The building officially opened the following year.

To the north at mile **3.6** you can see the Pan-Am pool built when the city hosted the Pan Am Games in 1967. It was again used when the city hosted the games in 1998. The western limits of Winnipeg are reached at mile **10.5** when you cross under the Perimeter Highway. On the south side of the tracks is a grain elevator named after the mileage (**10.6**).

Melville
280.3
272.1
266.4
258.3
257.8
245.1
239.0
234.9
Cana
Waldron
Bangor
Atwater
Zeneta
Yarbo
Cutarm
225.0
218.6
209.5
Spy Hill
Welby
Latimer
207.6
204.0
186.9
180.1
168.9
Raconville
St Lazare
Uno
Miniota
Stenberg
Oakner
159.4
149.2
143.2
137
Myra
Rivers
Levine
128.6
Brandon North

N

Isoboard plant outside Elie, Manitoba, turns unused straw into particle board.

Miles **10–27:** In this area, the *Canadian* passes some of the most fertile fields in North America. The water tower to the north, between miles **15.5** and **18**, is used by the Headingly Correctional facility.

Miles **28–50:** The rows of straw bales, to the north beginning at mile **28**, are used in the isoboard process. Inside the plant at mile **29**, the straw is dried, crushed, and then mixed with resins and pressed into boards for use in the furniture and construction industries. The town of Elie is passed at mile **32**. Look north to see the former station, now a private residence. The train parallels the Trans-Canada Highway, viewed to the north. The train again crosses the

Assiniboine River on a 125-metre (412-foot) long bridge at mile **50**.

Miles **51–58:** Portage la Prairie was named for the spot where the voyageurs rested before picking up their canoes and portaging over the prairie to Lake Manitoba, 22 kilometres (14 miles) to the north. At mile **53**, to the north is the Fort La Reine Museum featuring a replica of the fur trading outpost that La Verendrye used as his base for exploring the prairies, as well as a pioneer village and a railway display. Both railways serve Portage la Prairie. The yellow-bricked former CPR passenger station can be clearly seen across from the former CN station (mile **55**) now used by

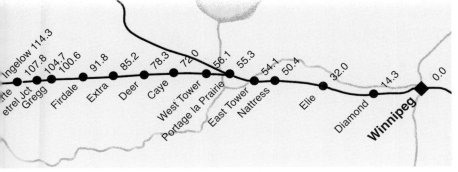

VIA. The station also doubles as the town's bus depot. Leaving town, you cross the CPR mainline which takes a more southern route. The immediate track to the north leads to what was originally the *Lake Manitoba Railway and Canal Company*. From a small stretch of track north of here, between Gladstone and Lake Manitoba, railway contractors Donald Mann and William Mackenzie began building the *Canadian Northern Railway*. It is also where VIA's *Hudson Bay*, detailed on page 111, turns north.

Miles **59–91:** When the Assiniboine River is ready to overflow its banks in Portage la Prairie, the Portage Diversion (mile **59**) carries water north to Lake Manitoba. The train crosses the Yellowhead highway at mile **63**, and then passes the Bloom fertilizer complex one mile later. Squirrel Creek is crossed at mile **83**.

Miles **92–97**: Ten thousand years ago, after glaciers receded to the north, a massive lake covered the majority of southern Manitoba. Here the *Canadian* winds through a scenic area that was once a series of beach ridges forming the western shores of the glacial Lake Agasis. The train crosses a scenic valley between miles **93.6** and **94.5**

Miles **98–126:** Now the train returns to farm terrain, as it moves through an area known for sunflower seeds and potatoes. Harte (mile **107**) was one of many communities on the prairies created at the point where steam locomotives would require more water. These watering stops had towers with special octagonal enclosures, designed to keep water from freezing in the winter. The old foundation of one of these can be seen here, as well as the old general store (now a private residence) with its antique gas pump.

Miles **127–140:** Brandon, Manitoba's second largest city, can be seen to the south while your train is stopped at Brandon North. Closer by, to the south-

The *Canadian* passes the fertile fields of the Red River Valley.

VIA's Canadian — Contact information on page 7

Crossing the large trestle at Uno, Manitoba, the *Canadian* snakes along the Assiniboine Valley.
— *Murray Hammond photo*

west of the highway, is the modern Agpro through-put grain elevator.

Miles **141–180:** The trestle at Rivers, Manitoba (mile **142**), carries the train 27 metres (90 feet) above the Little Saskatchewan River. The river was dammed to create Lake Wahtopanah, seen to the north. Rivers was the first *Grand Trunk Pacific* division point west of Winnipeg and the community displays CN Caboose 79528. Look to the south at mile **146** to view an airplane hanger used on the Rivers Air Base. The base was established by the British Commonwealth Air Training Plan during World War Two. The train crosses the Oak River at mile **148**.

Miles **181–213:** For all those who think the prairies are flat, the train winds through a cut in the terrain, and at mile **182** the scenic Assiniboine Valley appears on the south side of the tracks. The lazy Assiniboine River meanders along the valley floor creating oxbows, curved lanes made when the river silt cuts off previous curves in the river. At mile **185.6**, keep your camera ready for the

467-metre (1,533-foot) long Uno Trestle, 35 metres (115 feet) above the Minnewashtack Creek. The houses on the cliff at mile **189** are part of the Birdtail Creek First Nation. The valley widens and the train reaches its lowest point at St. Lazare (mile **204**), where it crosses the Assiniboine River once again. Mile **213** brings the train across the Manitoba/Saskatchewan border.

Mile **214–280:** To the south, between miles **214** and **216**, on the edge of the Qu'Appelle Valley, the Rocanville Potash Mine can be seen. Potash is used as fertilizer on many of the prairie farms. The town of Spy Hill (mile **225**) has a name based on a First Nations legend that tells of a dead Sioux man being left on a hill after being accused of spying on the local Cree. At mile **233** the train crosses the Big Cut Creek viaduct. The Cutarm Potash Mine, to the south at mile **234**, is connected to the Yarbo Mine to the north at mile **238** by the underground tunnel equivalent of a two-lane highway. The train arrives in Melville at mile **280**.

Route Highlights

Melville to Biggar
Watrous Subdivision

Miles 0–64: Melville is named after *Grand Trunk Pacific* President Charles Melville Hays, who perished on the *Titanic* after promoting the railway in England. The *Grand Trunk Pacific* had an interesting way of designating its station names in alphabetical order (excluding division points). This is emphasized as you pass through points like Fenwood (mile **12**), Goodeve (mile **18**), Hubbard (mile **28**), and Ituna (mile **34**), and so on.

Miles **65–105:** The scenic Touchwood Hills can be seen on both sides of the train between miles **65** and **75**. The Hudson Bay Company trading post, once situated on the north side of the tracks, was part of the firm's transport and provisioning network. The train crosses Peter Lake at mile **101**.

Miles **106–128:** The *Canadian* arrives at Nokomis, a name derived from Longfellow's poem Hiawatha. It was once also known as Junction City, since the GTP and CPR, and Highways 15 and 20, all met here. More of the community's history can be learned by visiting the Nokomis and District Museum, located in the former railway station (now situated in the centre of town). South of here is the large Last Mountain Lake, which has the oldest bird sanctuary in North America. Over 260 varieties of birds are found here, including the ferruginous hawk, white pelican, and whooping crane. Watch for these and more as the railway's right-of-way divides Boulder Lake in two at mile **117**.

Miles **129–188:** Watrous (mile **129**) is the starting point for visitors to Little Manitou Lake, located north of here. The lake is fed by underground springs and lies in a valley carved by receding glaciers. The Great Plains First Nation people always brought their sick to the "Lake of Good Spirit." The lake is more dense than the Dead Sea and has been long-believed to have recuperative powers. If nothing else, it provides a fun swim because it is impossible to sink.

When the settlers were staking their land, the bison, which once roamed the prairies in the millions, were becoming fewer and fewer. Early travellers would have seen piles of bleached bison bones along the tracks. They were collected from the land and sent east to be made into fertilizer. In fact, between 1890 and 1893, more than 3,200 rail cars of bison bones were shipped from Saskatoon alone. Look to the north to see the large

Zelma Reservoir between miles **146** and **149**. Between miles **177** and **178** the train passes through an area of smaller sloughs.

Miles **189–191**: Saskatoon is known as the "City of Bridges." One of the best views is featured to the north at mile **189** as The *Canadian* crosses the South Sas-

ity. If you wish to learn more about the province's rail history, we recommend a visit to the Saskatchewan Railway Museum. Everything from railway equipment to an interpretive building is featured at this six-acre attraction located just south of the city on Highway 60.

If you plan a visit anywhere in Saskatchewan, you can learn more by contacting Saskatchewan Tourism, 500-1900 Albert Street, Regina, SK S4P 4L9. Call: 800-667-7191. Web: *www.sasktourism.com*

127.7 | 122.2 | 114.1 | 106.2 | dora | Nokomis | Tate | 97.2 | Booth | 87.3 | Raymore | 82.9 | Quinton | 77.6 | Touchwood | 65.6 | Leross | 52.7 | Jasmin | 42.4 | Hubbard | 28.4 | Goodeve | 18.8 | Fenwood | 12.1 | Baily | 3.3 | Melville | 0.0

katchewan River on a 457-metre (1,500-foot) long bridge. Watch for the unique roof of the classic railway hotel, The Bessborough. Saskatoon's station is located in the railway yards in the southwest corner of the city, approximately 6.5 kilometres (4 miles) from the city centre.

Saskatoon was founded by a group of Ontario Methodists led by John Lake, who headed west to create a Temperance Colony based on their beliefs. The site he chose in 1883 has been transformed into Saskatchewan's largest city. Visitors will enjoy this oasis on the prairies by visiting everything from the Meewasin Valley Centre, featuring the city's history, to the Saskatoon branch of the Western Development Museums, Boomtown 1910, which features over 30 buildings from the area in an indoor facil-

For information on the city, we recommend you contact Tourism Saskatoon, 6 - 305 Idylwyld Drive North, Saskatoon, SK S7L 0Z1. Call: 800-567-2444.Web: *www. toursaskatoon .com*

Miles **192–246**: Carrying on past Saskatoon, the GTP system of naming towns in alphabetical order continues. Biggar, named after GTP official William H. Biggar, is reached at mile **247**. It was incorporated as a village in 1909. Around the same time, a local story tells of a group of surveyors pulling a prank one night by putting up a sign saying, "New York is big, but this is Biggar." The phrase stuck, and today it is featured in the town's emblem.

to the north between miles **89** and **90** to see Manitou Lake, which is unusual for a prairie lake because it features a large island in its centre. To the south, between miles **97** and **99**, Reflex Lake can be seen in a wooded setting.

Route Highlights
Biggar to Edmonton
Wainwright Subdivision

Miles 0–60: As you depart Biggar, look to the south to see a large roundhouse where steam locomotives were once serviced. Another style of railway buildings that have disappeared are interlocking towers that controlled train movements. These towers deployed a man who used a series of levers to control the railway switches. After Centralized Traffic Control (CTC) was introduced, hundreds of these towers were torn down. The one that controlled the crossing of the CP and CN near Oban (mile **9.3**) has been restored at the Saskatchewan Railway Museum in Saskatoon. The Killsquaw Lakes are passed on both sides of the tracks between miles **54** and **56**, before Unity is reached at mile **57**. At mile **59**, to the north, a grain elevator towers above a grove of trees. The *Canadian* then crosses under the tracks of a CPR branchline.

Miles **61–100:** The terrain here begins to change to rolling hills and small clumps of trees. The farm country changes from fields of wheat to large cattle ranches and grazing pastures. Look

The *Canadian* crosses the Saskatchewan/Alberta border at mile **101**.

Miles **102–138:** Oil was first discovered in this part of Alberta in the early 1920s; the area is still producing the black gold. Along the route for the next few miles, you will see numerous oil pumpjacks removing the crude from the ground. Burning off the methane gas helps new wells to start producing or to increase oil production. Chauvin (mile **106**) is a pretty town settled in the midst of rolling hills. While passing through Edgerton (mile **121**), notice the town historical society's heritage village. It features the Edgerton station and CNR caboose 79123, along with a school, the first United Church, and a display building for agriculture machinery. The town of Greenshields lives up to its name, as all the houses here are surrounded by fir trees.

Miles **139–145:** Approaching Wainwright, watch for peregrine falcons in

VIA's Canadian — Contact information on page 7

the sky as a breeding centre is nearby. The large rodeo grounds are busy every June with the annual fair. To the south you can see the railway equipment which makes up the Wainwright Railway Preservation Society. At mile **140** the town's large GTP-style station houses the Battle River Historical Society and Museum. The park behind the station reflects the community's rail heritage with CNR caboose 78492. Military equipment honours the major army training facility, Canadian Forces Base Camp Wainwright, which is located to the south.

184, owes its name to the Scandinavian settlers who founded the town in 1903. The station has been preserved by the Canadian Northern Society, which has preserved numerous stations in central Alberta. The park next to the station features a small replica of a Norse boat. You can look down the main street of Bruce, to the north, at mile **196**.

Miles **200–250:** While passing through Holden (mile **205**), look across the pond to see the elaborate silver dome of the Holy Ghost Ukrainian Catholic Church. Between miles **225** and **227** Beaverhill Lake can be seen to the north, only interrupted by Tofield at mile **226**. The train travels through a forested area and at mile **240**, passes Cooking Lake on the south. A former station from along the line lives on as

Miles **146–155:** At mile **146**, the Battle River Valley can first be seen to the north, on the other side of the community of Fabyan. Get your camera ready for the crossing of the Battle River Valley on a 886-metre (2,910-foot) long trestle at mile **149**. Excellent views are available from either side of the train. Once across the bridge, the train follows Grattan Creek to the south of the tracks until mile **154**.

Miles **155–199:** Highway 14, which is also known as the Poundmaker Trail, can be seen to the north. The *Canadian* will follow this highway for the rest of the way to Edmonton. Viking, at mile

the Junction Café on Highway 14, seen to the south at mile **244**.

Miles **251–264:** After a few miles of rolling hills, starting at mile **257**, the train passes Edmonton's numerous oil refineries and petroleum-related industries. Then, the train crosses high above the North Saskatchewan River on the Clover Bar Bridge (mile **260**). The large Edmonton Stockyards are on the north side of the tracks at mile **262**. Edmon-

Looking northwest over Alberta's Battle River Valley.

ton was one of the cities in Canada to see the benefits of transforming its commuter system by reintroducing a light rail transit system. The Belvedere Station, with its bright green roof, can be seen to the north at mile **263** before crossing the transit line. After this, the train enters the large Walker rail yards and the end of the subdivision. The train continues on the Edson Subdivision and crosses 97th Street. Look to the south over the Municipal Airport for a good view of Edmonton's business district. Arriving at the Edmonton Station, the train turns off the mainline on a wye and crosses the Yellowhead Trail before arriving at the terminal.

Edmonton is the provincial capital and features a variety of attractions, one of which is Fort Edmonton Park where four periods in the city's development are detailed. The modern Edmonton may best be experienced at the West Edmonton Mall with its indoor amusement park, submarine rides, and numerous shops. North of the City is the Alberta Railway Museum for those who want to learn more about the province's rail history. Located close to the Edmonton station is the Ramada Hotel and Conference Centre, 11834 Kingway. For reservations, call: 888-747-4114.

If you plan a visit anywhere in Alberta, you can learn more by contacting Travel Alberta, 10961 - 138th Street, Edmonton, AB T5M 1P3. Call: 888-414-4139. Web: *www.travelalberta.com*. For information on the city, we recommend you contact Edmonton Tourism, 9797 Jasper Avenue NW, Edmonton, AB T5J 1N9. Call: 800-661-8888. Web: *www.tourism.ede.org*

Route Highlights

Edmonton to Jasper
Edson Subdivision

Arriving or departing the Edmonton station, the train turns on a wye and crosses above the Yellowhead Trail before arriving at the terminal or back on the mainline.

Miles **4–18:** The train runs through an industrial area in Edmonton's northwest corner.

Miles **19–33:** If you need a hard-to-find part for your vehicle back home, you may want to spend some time in Spruce Grove's auto part yards. Stoney Plains, (mile **24**), features 16 large outdoor murals along its heritage Main Street. The picturesque Village of Carvel (mile **32.5**), with its General Store between the large fir trees and the silver dome of the Eastern Orthodox Church, is seen on the north side of the tracks. At mile **33** the *Canadian* curves around Mink Lake; the south side offers a fantastic opportunity to photograph your train. The train passes through the Wabamun First Nation Reserve at mile **38** and at mile **39** crosses Mink Creek.

Miles **43–53:** The large Wabamun Lake to the south is a popular weekend destination. The large Trans-Alta power plant sits on the north side of the tracks at mile **45**. This coal-powered plant's four units combine to burn 300 tonnes of coal per hour (equal to 72 train carloads per day) to power about 500,000 of the area's households. The Canadian Air Force once used the lake's large size to practice floatplane water landings.

Miles **54–122:** The former GTP Entwistle station is now a private residence; it can be seen on the north side of the tracks at mile **66**. At mile **67.6** the train crosses high above the Pembina River on a 274-metre (900-foot) long bridge. Chip Lake to the north at mile **78** can be seen intermittently behind the trees until mile **86**. The Lobstick River is crossed at mile **100** and Carrot Creek at mile **105**. The train then crosses two rivers within the same mile: McLeod River at **122.1**, then Sundance Creek at mile **122.6**.

Miles **123–151:** The train reaches Edson at mile **129**. Look to the south on the curved bridge at mile **136** to see the meandering Sundance Creek. At mile **139** the former Bikerdike station lives on as a farmhouse. As you reach

The Mink Lake curve at mile 33 of the Edson Sub offers a good opportunity to photograph your train.

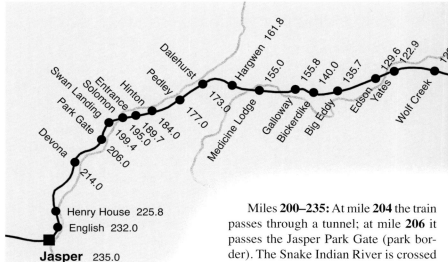

Henry House 225.8
English 232.0

Jasper 235.0

mile **151**, on a clear day you can get a distant view of the Miette Range of the Rocky Mountains to the south. Below is the rock-filled McLeod River.

Miles **152–184:** Travelling through the forested rolling hills, watch to the north for glimpses of the Athabasca Valley. The industrial town of Hinton, with a preserved GTP Station, is known as the "Gateway to the Rockies." While stopped here you get an extended view of the valley.

While crossing the Prairie Creek at mile **187**, look to the north to see where it flows into the Athabasca River.

Miles **193-199**: The train crosses the Athabasca River (mile **193**) on a 189-metre (620-foot) long bridge. The river's unique blue colour comes from the sunlight reflecting off the rock silt in the water. The river continues on the south side of the tracks before it widens at mile **196** to form Lake Brule. The lake was named after explorer Etienne Brule, who travelled this river route after fellow explorers David Thompson and Alexander Mackenzie.

Miles **200–235:** At mile **204** the train passes through a tunnel; at mile **206** it passes the Jasper Park Gate (park border). The Snake Indian River is crossed at mile **211**. Jasper House, a fur trading supply post built in 1813, was named after Jasper Hawes; it was located on the opposite side of Jasper Lake at mile **215**. The causeway at mile **217** was a popular spot to take promotional photos of CN's *Super Continental*. Mountain goats are a common sight on the steep rocks on the north side of the tracks. Snaring River is crossed at mile **225**, Another supply station, Henry House, lies between Jasper Lake and the rails at mile **225.8**. Watch for elk in this area. The train arrives at the picturesque Jasper Station at mile **235**. There is an extended stop here so you have a chance to stretch your legs, browse the gift shops along Connaught Drive, and photograph yourself beside CNR steam locomotive 6015.

Originally known as Fitzhugh, the town's name was changed to Jasper in 1911. Until the 1930s they only way to get to this remote park town was by horse or train. Today, situated in the middle of Jasper National Park, the growth of the town is strictly limited, but there is more than enough to see and do to keep you busy for days. If you are plan-

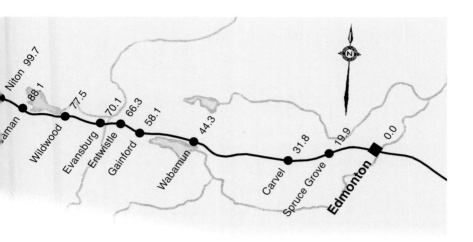

Niton 99.7
88.1
Wildwood
77.5
Evansburg
70.1
Entwistle
66.3
Gainford
58.1
Wabamun
44.3
Carvel 31.8
Spruce Grove 19.9
Edmonton 0.0

ning a few days here, or are transferring to VIA's *Skeena* (detailed on page 120), we recommend the walking tour of the town site presented by the Friends of Jasper National Park. At the Jasper-Yellowhead Museum and Archives, you can learn more about the Tent City resort that was set up for visitors on the shores of Lac Beauvert.

Today the same site is occupied by the Jasper Park Lodge. Built by the *Canadian National Railways*, this world class resort, with its separate cabins, is managed today by Fairmont Hotels. Cab shuttles depart from the station to take passengers to the lodge. Reservations can be made at: 800-441-1414. Web: *www.fairmont.com*. If they are booked and you wish to stay in town, a popular alternative is private home accommodation. For this we recommend the spacious two-bedroom suite of the Homestead at 23 Aspen Crescent. Contact your friendly hosts Harry and Edna Home at: 780-852-5818.

Many photo opportunities are available as the train passes the mountain ranges of the Canadian Rockies near Jasper, Alberta.

Route Highlights

Jasper to Blue River
Albreda Subdivision

Miles 0–16: On the west side of Jasper between miles **2** and **3**, Whistler Mountain can be clearly seen on the south side of the tracks. The small building on the mountaintop is the upper terminal of the Jasper aerial tramway 2,500 metres (8,202 feet) above sea level. At mile **6** the train passes slide detector fences. Seen in numerous spots along the tracks, these fences warn trains if rock slides or boulders have fallen, potentially blocking the tracks. When the wires are broken, a signal is automatically sent to the train to stop. Between miles **11** and **15** watch the small ponds and clearings for moose. At mile **16** there is a good curve on which to photograph your train.

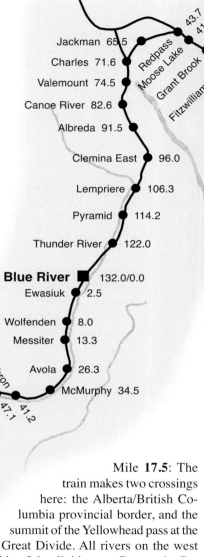

Jackman 65.5
Charles 71.6
Valemount 74.5
Canoe River 82.6
Albreda 91.5
Redpass
Moose Lake
Grant Brook
Fitzwilliam 2
43.7
41.6
Clemina East 96.0
Lempriere 106.3
Pyramid 114.2
Thunder River 122.0
Blue River 132.0/0.0
Ewasiuk 2.5
Wolfenden 8.0
Messiter 13.3
Avola 26.3
McMurphy 34.5
Clearwater
Birch Island
Vavenby
Irvine
Wabron
67.0
61.6
53.0
47.1
41.2
Blackpool 73.8
Boulder 83.0
N
Chu Chua 90.9
Chinook Cove 98.0
Barriere 104.4
Exlou 108.2
McLure 115.8
Vinsulla 123.7
Mackenzie 134.3
Batchelor 135.8
Kamloops 139.0

Mile **17.5**: The train makes two crossings here: the Alberta/British Columbia provincial border, and the summit of the Yellowhead pass at the Great Divide. All rivers on the west side of the divide now flow to the Pacific. The border is also the boundary for Jasper National Park on the Alberta side and Mt. Robinson Provincial Park on the British Columbia side. You also cross the line between the Mountain and Pacific Time Zones. Move your travel clocks and watches one hour back if travelling west, or one hour forward if travelling east.

VIA's Canadian — Contact information on page 7

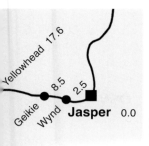

Miles 18–37: Scenic Yellowhead Lake is passed at miles **21–22** to the south. Fitzwilliam Mountain can be seen on the left, and Mount Rockingham to the right, on the opposite side of the lake. On the south side of the tracks at mile **24** is the beginning of the Fraser River. The train crosses Grant Brook at mile **31** and Moose River at mile **33**.

Miles 38–43: Between the railway and the Selwyn Mountain Range sits Moose Lake. Watch for the tall waterfalls on the opposite shore. At mile **43** is Red Pass Junction; this is where the *Grand Trunk Pacific* (which was parallel to the *Canadian Northern* route) turned to the west for Prince Rupert, while the *Canadian Northern* continued on a southwest course for Vancouver. (Turn to page 120 for details on VIA's *Skeena*.).

Miles 44–71: The Fraser River is the next river crossed. The tracks on the highline are located on a ledge above the former GTP line. The train goes through a tunnel at mile **48**, then crosses Glacier Creek at mile **50.5** and Snowslide Creek at mile **51.8**. If the runoff level of the water is high, the falls can be quite dramatic. Between miles **58** and **63** watch to the north of the tracks to see the tallest mountain in the Canadian Rockies, Mount Robson, at a towering 3,954 metres (12,972 feet) above sea level. On the south side of the tracks is Mount Terry Fox, named for the courageous one-legged young man who set out on his 1980 Marathon of Hope to run across Canada to raise funds for cancer research. In a few miles, the tracks turn to the south. The mountain range to the northwest is known as the Premier Range, since the mountain peaks are named for Canadian prime ministers. The Robson Subdivision connects with the Albreda Subdivision at mile **71**.

Miles 72–113: At mile **74** the train passes through Valemount. Main Street is located on the south side of the track, and features a hotel with the Log-n-Rail Bar (which hints at the town's two largest employers). A museum is located in the former station, beside CN Caboose 79726, next to the log building housing the town library. Good views of mountains to all sides occur between miles **76** and **80**. As the train crosses the Canoe River at mile **80.6**, you pass a small cairn that marks the spot where soldiers enroute to Korea died in a railway mishap on November 21, 1950. River crossings continue with the Clemina River at mile **97** and Cascade Creek at mile **102**. Look to the north side of the tracks for the white picket fence marking the grave of a railway worker who died during the line's construction. The North Thompson River, on the north side of the tracks, should be visible in this area. Serpentine Creek is crossed at mile **110**.

Mile 113.5: Have your camera ready, because the spectacular Pyramid Falls can be seen to the south. The water of Pyramid Creek hits a unique outcropping of rock to create a triangular effect. Below the falls, the creek passes under the tracks.

Miles 114–132: The train crosses the North Thompson River at mile **123.1** and Thunder River at mile **123.4**. Then at mile **131**, the Blue River is crossed. Look to the south while on the bridge for good views. Finally, you reach Blue River at mile **132**.

Route Highlights

Blue River to Kamloops
Clearwater Subdivision

Miles 0–44: The snowcapped mountains change to large rolling hills east of Blue River. At mile **8** the train begins to travel through the narrow North Thompson River Canyon, then crosses Berry Creek three times. At mile **12** watch to the south for the gorge and rushing water of Little Hell's Gate Canyon. Then the train enters a tunnel. The area below Groundhog Mountain is known for its rockslides. More slide detectors are passed starting at mile **17**. Cottonwood trees line the banks of the area's rivers. The train crosses the North Thompson River on a 107-metre (352-foot) long bridge at mile **32**, then the Otter Creek at mile **33**. Look to the north at miles **42** and **43** to see the Mad River Rapids. Good views are offered when the North Thompson is again crossed at mile **44**. You are following the same route taken by the gold rush "Overlanders" in 1862 — well before the coming of the railway — when over 200 people travelled from eastern Ontario and Quebec to Kamloops to start a new life.

Miles 45–139: The train now travels through a region of sandy cliffs and soil. It crosses the North Thompson at mile **59.1** and **59.5**. The community of Birch Island at mile **61** can be seen both on the opposite shore and on Butchers Island in the middle of the North Thompson. At mile **68** watch for the Clearwater River flowing into the North Thompson. At mile **103** the train crosses Barriere River and, at mile **107**, Lois Creek. Look to the north at mile **114** to see Fishtrap Rapids. You reach Rayleigh, a northern suburb of Kamloops, at mile **131**. Look on the opposite side of the river to see the suburb of Westsyde. Kamloops is next reached. The station is located in the northern part of this large BC-interior city. From the station, look to see the suburbs rising out of the hills on the south side of the city. If you are planning to spend some time in the city where the North and South Thompson Rivers meet, we recommend you contact the Kamloops Visitor Info Centre, 1290 West Trans-Canada Highway, Kamloops, BC V2C 6R3. Call: 800-662-1994.

The tallest mountain in the Canadian Rockies, Mount Robson, seen as dawn breaks in the winter months.

VIA's Canadian — Contact information on page 7

Route Highlights

Kamloops to Boston Bar
Ashcroft Subdivision

When the Canadian Northern Railway construction crews reached Kamloops in 1913, the Canadian Pacific had already chosen the easier sides of the Thompson and Fraser River Canyons to build its line to the Pacific. So the Canadian Northern had no choice but to build on the opposite banks.

Miles **0–6:** Departing Kamloops the train crosses the North Thompson River. The train then travels through the suburb of Brocklehurst.

Miles **7–25:** The Thompson River widens to form Kamloops Lake. Birds are plentiful in the arid landscape, including killdeer, mallards, spotted sandpiper, and osprey, which have their large nests in the area. The lake disappears from view when you pass through the numerous tunnels, beginning with the Tranquile tunnel at mile **9**, then the Battle Bluff tunnel at mile **10**. The CPR also had to build tunnels on the south side; at mile **11** look to the south to see the five Cherry Creek tunnels. At mile **20** the train enters the Copper Creek tunnel. Savona can be seen on the opposite side of the lake, before it narrows to form the Thompson River.

Miles **26–49:** The desolate Deadman's Valley can be seen to the north. The train crosses the Thompson River numerous times over the next few miles, beginning at mile **28** on a 227-metre (745-foot) long bridge, then back to the north side at mile **34** on a 335-metre (1,110-foot) long bridge. After a few miles the train crosses the river again at mile **45.8**. Once across, look to the north to see Rattlesnake Hill before

the train returns to the north shore at mile **47**. At mile **47.9** look for the white post that marks the height of the water level in 1880 after a rockslide dammed the river. The town of Ashcroft (mile **48**) is known as one of the driest places in Canada.

Miles **50–74:** At mile **51** the train passes through a tunnel and emerges on the other side amidst the volcanic rock of Black Canyon. The curve at mile **52** provides a good opportunity to photograph your train. The train crosses the river at mile **55** and passes through tunnels alongside the CPR.

Mile **57:** Some of the heaviest rail traffic in the country occurs between here at Basque and Mission to the south. Trains travelling eastward from Vancouver may travel on the Canadian Pacific line from Mission until returning to the Canadian National line here.

Miles **58–74:** At mile **59** the CN line crosses back to the north side of the river. On January 23, 1915, in a simple ceremony, the last spike on the Canadian Northern Pacific was driven near mile **63**. The train enters the Martel tunnels at miles **67.5** and **67.6**. Spences Bridge, at mile **74**, is named for the man who built a toll bridge over the Nicola River in 1864 for the Caribou Trail.

Miles **75–96:** Master anglers visit this area of the river every year for some of the world's best steelhead fishing. The area is also known for its big horn sheep. The train enters Rainbow Canyon, named for the various colours of this gorge's steep walls. At mile **80** you pass through three tunnels and four rock sheds. The rapids on the river here are popular with whitewater rafters. On the CPR side, note the Indictment Hole trestle at mile **86**. At mile **87** you can see

Nikomen Falls deep in its own gorge. There is a stone arch bridge at mile **90**. As well, look to the river to see the Suicide Rapids, here at the Jaws of Death Gorge. Note how the canyon seems to be lit up with the various colours of the rocks. The view is marred between miles **93** and **94** when the train passes through numerous tunnels, rocksheds, and a flume.

Miles **97–104:** Lytton can be seen on the opposite side of the river. At mile **97.4** the train crosses the Fraser River. Look below and to the west to see the blue-green water of the Thompson mix with the dark, silt-laden water of the Fraser. At mile **98.3** to the east, you can see a small First Nations cemetery. At mile **103** the railways once again trade sides in the most impressive way at Cisco, so named for a First Nations word that translates to "unpredictable." The CN crosses on a 247-metre (810-foot) long bridge over 60 meters (200 feet) above the swirling waters. The CPR bridge can be seen to the south. Both bridges can be seen from the south shore at mile **104.**

Miles **105–125:** At mile **105** look to the west to see the looming Pinnacle Rock. At mile **109** the train enters a long tunnel through Jackass Mountain, named for the stubborn but sturdy mules that carried so much equipment on the Caribou Road. Good views come at mile **120** where the train crosses the Ainslie Creek, 42 metres (140 feet) below. The train crosses Stoyoma Creek on a 232-metre (763-foot) long bridge before reaching Boston Bar. The name of this community comes from the time when many of the gold seekers ventured into this area from Boston, Massachusetts, in search of the elusive mineral.

Route Highlights

Boston Bar to New Westminster Yale Subdivision

Miles 0–6: At mile **4** the train passes Skuzzy Creek, on the opposite shore. It is not named for its water, but for the only sternwheeler that did what was thought to be impossible. *Skuzzy*, built in 1882, was commissioned by railway contractor Andrew Onderdonk to bring supplies to assist with the building of the Dominion Government portion of the *Canadian Pacific Railway*. To get past the rapids, ringbolts were driven into the river's rock walls. Ropes attached to the boat were then passed through the rings and, with the steamship working its hardest, men pulled on the ropes. Thus, *Skuzzy* became the only sternwheeler to navigate through and beyond Hell's Gate Rapids.

Mile 7: The rapids at Hell's Gate were altered in 1914 when the *Canadian Northern* blasted too much rock away while building its new line. This narrowed the gorge and fish ladders had to be built to assist spawning salmon. Above here are the red cars of the Hells

Gate airtram; below you, the river surges to its narrowest point—only 35 metres (110 feet) across. During every minute, 200 million gallons of water rushes past at approximately 28 km per hour (17 mph). Take your photos before you enter a tunnel at mile **7.2**.

Miles 8–40: The train passes through a series of tunnels between miles **8** and **9** and then at mile **11**. At mile **21.5** the rock formation in the middle of river is called Steamboat Island. You reach Yale at mile **26**—watch the river for the large black Lady Franklin Rock. This marks

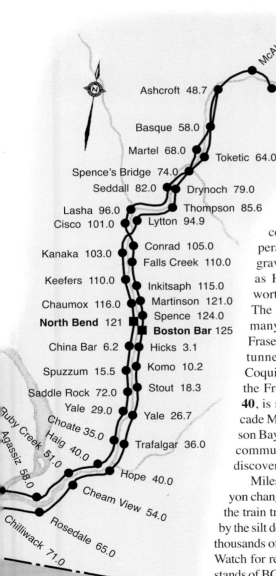

the spot where the wife of noted explorer Sir John Franklin could travel no further in her desperate search for her husband. The gravel shore near mile **28** is known as Hill's Bar; in 1875, $2 million worth of gold was discovered here. The Suka Creek at mile **30** is one of many in the area that flow into the Fraser. The train passes through another tunnel at mile **35**, then crosses the Coquihalla River (where it empties into the Fraser at mile **39.8**). Hope, at mile **40**, is surrounded by the beautiful Cascade Mountains; it was originally a Hudson Bay outpost known as Fort Hope. The community blossomed when gold was discovered in the region.

Miles 41–59: The rugged Fraser Canyon changes to the Fraser Valley. But before the train travels through the fertile fields left by the silt deposited from the Fraser River over thousands of years, you pass some lush forests. Watch for red and orange elderberry trees and stands of BC's shaggy maple; cottonwood trees

The Fraser River's Hells Gate Rapids as seen from the comfort of the train.

are visible, as are dogwoods with their twisted trunks. Once clear of the forests and into the agricultural area you pass dairy farms and fields full of produce for market gardens. The area is known to some as "the food basket for Vancouver." At mile **59**, look to the south to see the Skagit Mountain Range and Cheam Peak.

Miles **60–88:** Watch for glimpses of the Fraser River to the north. Chilliwack, at mile **71.8**, was originally known as Centreville. The community grew with the gold rush when passengers transferred from the riverboats to the new community on the shore of the Fraser. This milk-producing region, with its large dairy barns, is home to holstein, jersey, and guernsey cows. At mile **77**, the train crosses the Sumas River on a 138-metre (455-foot) bridge. While passing through Matsqui, look to the north from miles **84** to **86** to see the hill with Westminster Abbey and its high steeple.

Mile **89:** At Page all eastbound passenger trains connect to the *Canadian Pacific* mainline and cross the Fraser on the Mission bridge. The train then travels on the north side of the Fraser until it reconnects to the CN mainline at Basque.

Miles **90–117:** The Fraser, now much wider and with large islands, can be seen between the trees. At mile **101** the train passes the Fort Langley airfield. Fort Langley was originally a Hudson Bay Company fort, built in 1827 to serve the area of New Caledonia and Columbia Districts (now British Columbia and northern Washington). Today the replica of this fort is a National Historic Site; it can be seen along the tracks at mile **102**. Also here is the former CN station that now serves as home for the Langley Heritage Society, a tourist information centre, and an art gallery (in the freight shed). On the grounds is a restored caboose, with a model railway display, and a restored 1947 passenger coach. At mile **108**, you see Douglas Island in the middle of the Fraser River. Bungalow Y is the CN intermodal yard serving Vancouver; cargo containers are transferred here. Between miles **113** and **114**, to the south and above, you see where the Trans-Canada Highway crosses the Fraser on the Port Mann Bridge. The train passes through the CN Thornton Yards at mile **116**.

Mile **118:** The Fraser River Bridge is the longest crossing your train will make over the Fraser. New Westminster sits on the north shore, and Surrey sits on the south side. The bridge your train is crossing was built in the early 1900s. It can swing open to allow large ships to pass through. Above it is the Pattullo vehicle bridge. Beyond that is a large suspension bridge for the sole use of the *Skytrain*, Vancouver's automated light-rail mass transit system.

Route Highlights

New Westminster to Vancouver
New Westminster Subdivision

The train runs on tracks operated by the *Burlington Northern Santa Fe* (successor to the *Great Northern Railway*) as it travels through Vancouver.

On the south side of the river the tracks run parallel to the river; the New Westminster station and yard office can be seen to the east. As the track turns sharply, look above to see the *Skytrain* Braid Station.

The south side of the track forms the border of the Burnaby Lake Nature Park. The train then travels the next couple of miles through an industrial area.

After that, in a scene reminiscent of the tracks that travel through Halifax, the train travels through the Great Northern Cut, passing under Nanaimo Street, Lakewood Drive, Victoria Drive, Broadway Avenue East, Commercial Drive (where the *Skytrain* parallels the route above), Woodland Drive, and Clark Drive.

The track opens into another industrial area. If you are travelling westbound, the train is "wyed" (turned around) before you back into the western terminus of Vancouver's Pacific Central Station, built in 1919. In front of this grand station is Thornton Park and the Main Street stop of Vancouver's efficient *Skytrain* mass transit system.

You will need more than a few days to take in this spectacular city's sights. We recommend the Fairmont Hotel Vancouver, located in the heart of the city at 900 West Georgia Street. This is another classic railway hotel, which has welcomed guests since 1887. It is actually the third hotel that bears same the name, and was built on this site in 1939. You will enjoy its grand elegance, commitment to service, and comfortable rooms after a long day of sightseeing or business. Reservations can be made at: 800-441-1414 or 604-684-313. Web: *www.fairmont.com*

This area, where the mountains meet the sea, was home to the Haida First Nations people. The first European to explore this beautiful coast was Captain James Cook, who arrived in 1778. Captain George Vancouver, who had made the trip with Cook fourteen years earlier, returned in 1792 and explored the area for two years.

New Westminster was the first seaport, thanks to gold being discovered along the shores of the Fraser River. Vancouver traces its origins to a few entrepreneurs who started some industries on an unspoiled strip of land nearby, along the Burrard Inlet. A shantytown sprung up in the area. In 1867, a retired sailor-turned-bar-owner named Gassy Jack Leighton opened a drinking establishment. Soon thereafter the area was known as Gassy's Town. This name did not last long; after a couple of years the name of the growing community was changed to Granville. *Canadian Pacific Railway* changed the name to Vancouver in 1884 when it chose the site as its western terminus. The new city has continued to grow ever since the first steam locomotive pulled in from Montreal in 1887. Today this vibrant city on Canada's west coast is one of the country's favourite destinations.

The *Skytrain* terminal is the former *Canadian Pacific Railway* station now known as Waterfront Station. This is also the terminal for the *West Coast Express* commuter train to Mission, and the cross-bay *Seabus* to West Vancouver. A short distance from here is Vancouver's "Gastown," with its charming old buildings featuring restaurants, boutiques, and a Steam Clock that has been a popular attraction since it was refurbished in 1977. Do not miss Stanley Park, where you can enjoy its eight-kilometre walking trail around the park, or the Vancouver Aquarium and Science Centre. Chinatown, with its busy streets and the tranquil Dr. Sun Yat-Sen Classical Chinese Garden, is an interesting area to visit. Across town, on the south side of False Creek, you will find the renovated warehouses of Granville Island Market featuring everything from fresh seafood to an art school. At False Creek you can jump on an Aquabus and travel to Drake Street on the opposite shore. This area was once a railway yard, and became the site of Expo 86. The glass pavilion attached to the Roundhouse Community Centre houses CPR locomotive 374. Here you can reflect back on your rail trip, and think about the journey experienced by those aboard the first transcontinental train that arrived in Vancouver on May 23, 1887.

Before you visit Vancouver, we recommend you contact Tourism Vancouver at 210-200 Burrard Street, Vancouver, BC V6C 3L6. Call: 604-683-2000. Web: *www.tourismvancouver.com*

If you plan on visiting anywhere else in the province, you can contact Super Natural British Columbia at Stn, Prov, Govt, Victoria, BC V8W 9W5. Call: 800-HELLO BC. Web: *www.hellobc.com*

The end of the journey and Vancouver's Pacific Central Station.

Hudson Bay Route

The railway to Churchill was first conceived as a way to break the monopoly that forced farmers to ship their grain via the west coast or Thunder Bay. Today, it provides travellers with an opportunity to journey northward to Hudson Bay. Here for 3000 years, indigenous people have led a nomadic life. European visitors date back to 1619, when the Danish Munk expedition wintered here while searching for the Northwest Passage. Tie-down rings can still be seen in the rocks near the mouth of the Churchill River. Also remaining today is the majestic Fort Prince of Wales, dating back to 1700.

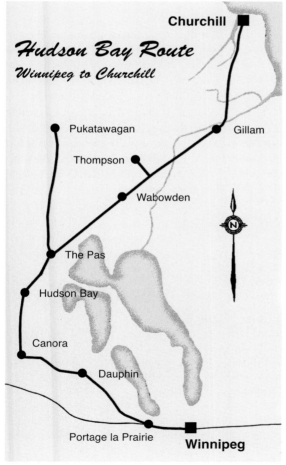

Hudson Bay Company trappers and traders started from the north, and travelled south to expand the fur trade. Travellers today on VIA Rail's *Hudson Bay* can begin in Winnipeg and travel the 1,697 kilometres (1,060 miles) in considerable comfort. The untouched scenery along the route can be full of surprises, no matter what time of year you take this journey.

The train departs Winnipeg and initially follows the route of the *Canadian*, detailed on page 90, turning north from the Rivers Subdivision at mile **55.7** in Portage la Prairie.

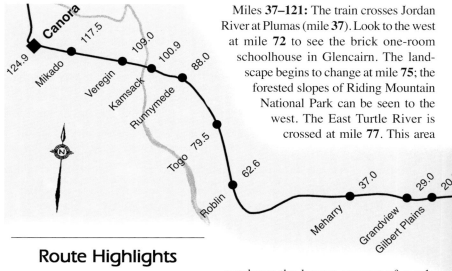

Miles **37–121:** The train crosses Jordan River at Plumas (mile **37**). Look to the west at mile **72** to see the brick one-room schoolhouse in Glencairn. The landscape begins to change at mile **75**; the forested slopes of Riding Mountain National Park can be seen to the west. The East Turtle River is crossed at mile **77**. This area

Route Highlights

Portage La Prairie to Dauphin
Gladstone Subdivision

Miles 0–37: The big sky country scenery of the picturesque prairies continues to be evident along the route. When the Assiniboine River (located to the south of here) is ready to overflow its banks in Portage la Prairie, water is carried north to Lake Manitoba by the Portage Diversion (crossed at mile **3.7**). The train crosses Beaver Creek at mile **19**, followed by Squirrel Creek (mile **24**), and Pine Creek (mile **29**). Dead Lake can be seen on both sides of the track at mile **34**, before arriving in Gladstone. Here the train travels surprisingly close to some of the town's buildings. The CN tracks parallel and then cross the CPR Minnedosa Subdivision at mile **37** before traversing the White Mud Creek. In 1895 William Mackenzie and Donald Mann purchased the *Lake Manitoba Railway and Canal Company* for its Gladstone north to Sifton railway charter. From this simple beginning, Canada's second transcontinental railway, the *Canadian Northern Railway*, began.

produces the largest amount of maple syrup in Western Canada. A traditional prairie station remains in McCreary at mile **83**. The train travels northwest through fields and forests, passing through Laurier at mile **92** and Makinak at mile **100**. At mile **108** the train crosses Ochre River in the town of the same name. At mile **121**, you arrive in the city of Dauphin, with its unique brick station and former station garden (now a park). The city is a popular starting point for visits to Riding Mountain National Park to the south.

Crossing the Assiniboine River near Portage la Prairie, Manitoba.

Route Highlights

Dauphin to Canora
Togo Subdivision

Miles 0–77: Beside the station is preserved CNR caboose 79727. The former railway locomotive roundhouse, seen on the south side of the tracks at mile **1**, lives on as the City of Dauphin Public Works garage. Continuing due west, the train passes large farms, with Riding Mountain in the distance to the south. The former station in Gilbert Plains at mile **20** has been moved slightly north to the corner of Main and Gordon, where it lives on as a senior's centre. When you see the incredible view to the south of Grandview (mile **29**), you will understand how this prairie town got its name. Watch to the north side of the tracks to see the heritage buildings and the large grey sheds that house the antique cars and farm implements of the Watson Crossley Community Museum.

The train continues to wind around this parkland region, reaching Roblin station at mile **62**. Built in 1900, this station has been transformed into Abigail's at the Station, which features homemade crafts, tourist information, and a heritage tea-room.

Miles **79–124:** Instead of a trestle bridge the train crosses a large earth fill at mile **92** and winds through an area of rolling hills before arriving at Kamsack (mile **100**). The Assiniboine River is crossed at mile **101**, before the tracks curve away from town. Veregin (mile **109**) was formed by a group of Doukhobours who left Russia and followed Peter Veregin to settle here in 1899. The National Doukhobour Heritage Village sits behind the grain elevators on the west side of the tracks. The Canora station at mile **124** is now a museum that features a CNR yard caboose. Look into the station's bay window—it appears that the telegrapher has just stepped away for a moment.

Harrington 4.0

21.7 ■ **Dauphin**

Ochre River ● 108.0

Makinak ● 100.0

Laurier ● 92.4

McCreary ● 83.0

Glencairn ● 72.5

Glenella ● 63.8

Colby ● 48.0

37.4 ● Plumas

36.5 ● Gladstone

31.2 ● Golden Stream

18.6 ● Beaver

9.9 ● Rignold

0.6 ● Delta Jct

Portage la Prairie

Route Highlights

Canora to Hudson Bay
Assiniboine Subdivision

Miles 0–92: Arriving in Sturgis at mile **21**, the train will cross the Assiniboine River. On the hill where the town is, you can catch a glimpse of the former railway station,

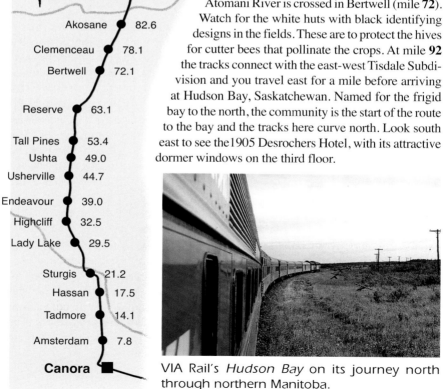

The Pas   88.1
The Pas South   83.4
Westray   68.3
Whithorn   60.5
Turnberry   50.6
Otosquien   35.2
Chemong   27.2
Ceba   17.9
Relitz   1.8
Hudson Bay   92.2
Akosane   82.6
Clemenceau   78.1
Bertwell   72.1
Reserve   63.1
Tall Pines   53.4
Ushta   49.0
Usherville   44.7
Endeavour   39.0
Highcliff   32.5
Lady Lake   29.5
Sturgis   21.2
Hassan   17.5
Tadmore   14.1
Amsterdam   7.8
Canora

now a museum, and a small terrace at the end of the main street overlooking the track and river. The train passes Highcliff at mile **32**, Endeavour at mile **39,** and Usherville at mile **44**. You will know how Tall Pines at mile **53** received its name when you see the towering trees here. The Atomani River is crossed in Bertwell (mile **72**). Watch for the white huts with black identifying designs in the fields. These are to protect the hives for cutter bees that pollinate the crops. At mile **92** the tracks connect with the east-west Tisdale Subdivision and you travel east for a mile before arriving at Hudson Bay, Saskatchewan. Named for the frigid bay to the north, the community is the start of the route to the bay and the tracks here curve north. Look south east to see the 1905 Desrochers Hotel, with its attractive dormer windows on the third floor.

VIA Rail's *Hudson Bay* on its journey north through northern Manitoba.

Overlooking the "Gateway to the North," The Pas, Manitoba.

Route Highlights

Hudson Bay to The Pas
Turnberry Subdivision

Miles 0–49: Travelling northwest, the train departs Hudson Bay. Between miles **7** and **8**, on the west side of the tracks, the train passes Ruby Lake and Ruby Beach Provincial Park. Then you travel through a thickly-forested area. The Saskatchewan/Manitoba border is crossed at mile **49**.

Miles **50–88:** The train crosses the Pasquia River at mile **50**. Then at mile **68** it crosses Highway No. 10, and begins to parallel the highway at mile **71**. Getting closer to The Pas, you pass through the most northerly agricultural area in the province, the Carrot River Valley.

History repeats itself through the railway's name. Originally known as the *Hudson Bay Railway,* it later became part of *Canadian National Railways,* owned by the federal government. It was sold to OmniTrax in 1997, who reclaimed the original name, and is again known as the *Hudson Bay Railway.*

At mile **87** the train curves into the town's railway yard. Looking to the east you see the white 5-stall railway roundhouse (if it is not obscured by freight cars) before arriving at The Pas station.

Known as the "Gateway to the North" there has been evidence of people residing here as far back as 5,000 years. The Pas can trace its first European visitor back to July 5, 1691, when Hudson Bay explorer Henry Kelsey passed through. When Sir John Franklin went missing in the arctic while searching for the North West Passage, the Richardson search party spent the winter here in 1847 and 1848. Some of the members of that party were carpenters who carved the pews still used in the local Anglican church today. In 1908 the *Canadian Northern Railway* arrived. The Community Building and Court House added to the growing community when completed in 1917. Today, the building houses the Sam Waller Museum.

If you are planning to spend some time here, possibly to take the Puckatawagen wayfreight (mixed freight and passenger train) for a wilderness paddling trip, you might see the unique blue cars used for this train outside the station. We recommend the convenient Wescana Inn, a short distance from the station at 439 Fischer Avenue. Reservations can be made at: 800-665-9468. For tourism information, call: 866-627-1134. Web: *www.thepasarea.com*

Route Highlights

The Pas to Wabowden
Wekusko Subdivision

Miles 0–136: The tracks curve through the town as they depart The Pas. Look to the west to see the steeple of Our Lady of the Sacred Heart Cathedral opposite St. Anthony's Hospital. You also pass Devon Park with a preserved CNR Caboose, and the Skippy L, which was built in 1936 by The Pas Canoe Company, then worked the Saskatchewan River and its tributaries for over 40 years. At mile **0.6** you cross this impressive river on a 259-metre (850-foot) long bridge. On the north side of the river, to the east, you pass the Opaskwayak First Nation Reserve and the Otineka Mall and the Aseneskak Casino in the distance. To the east the large Tolko lumber and pulp and paper

complex is passed at mile **3**. Then the Flin Flon Junction, where the Lynn Lake wayfreight continues west, is passed at mile **4.2**. On the north side of the tracks sits Clearwater Lake Provincial Park. The lake itself can be glimpsed between the trees at mile **16.9**. The interesting tripod telegraph poles, now retired in place, were built because standard poles sunk in the ground would be pushed out after time by the permafrost. Keep your camera ready to photograph the beautiful Cormorant Lake (miles **32-35**), an area known for its waterfowl and a place

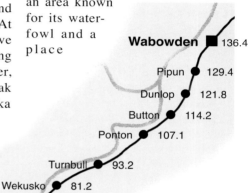

where more than one fishing legend has been caught.

At mile **38.9** on the west side of the tracks, you can see a former pink marble quarry. Then you arrive in the community of Cormorant (mile **41**) and cross the narrows that connect to Little Cormorant Lake on the east side.

Miles **85–87**: Look to the east to see Hargrave Lake. The landscape changes the further north you go. Wabowden, with its old station and row of buildings, is reached at mile **136.**

Hudson Bay Route — Contact information on page 7

Route Highlights

Wabowden to Gillam
Thicket Subdivision

Mile 136–326: Mile **143** offers a good curve to photograph your train. Thicket Portage (mile **184**) was where the Franklin Expedition rested before continuing north. The unique white pipes sticking out of the ground at miles **196** and **197** are thermal pipes. They help to prevent sinkholes by keeping the ground under the tracks frozen in the spring as long as possible.

At mile **199** the train takes a short diversion on the Thompson Subdivision. This was built to connect the main line to the location of a large deposit of nickel where the town of Thompson was emerging, and was completed when the premier of Manitoba, Douglas Campbell, drove home a spike of solid nickel on October 20, 1957. You see a mine head on the south side of the tracks at mile **28.8**, before you arrive at Thompson station at mile **30.5**.

Returning to the Thicket Subdivision and continuing north, the train arrives at Pikwitonei (mile **213**), and crosses the river of the same name. At mile **225** the tracks cross Lake Armstrong. When building the line, the railway dumped endless amounts of fill to cross the lake. Eventually, a small steam locomotive and some flat cars slid into the lake. Watch on the east side of the tracks to see this train when the water is low. Mile **238** was once the site of a sawmill, but it is now where native hunters and trappers leave the train for a trail that leads to the Nelson River. At mile **240** the train curves through a rock cut and crosses the Nelson on a 186-metre (612-foot) long bridge 31 metres (100 feet) above the river. The train passes Spring Lake to the east at mile **255**, then crosses Landing River at mile **278**. Near the station in Ilford (mile **285**) sits a Linn tractor. This is a tribute to the days when the town was a transfer point from rail to winter tractor trains for transportation onward to God's Lake gold fields 130 miles to the southeast. Gillam (mile **326**) has a large station and a display of a 23-ton locomotive and a caboose used during the construction of the area's hydroelectric projects. This is the end of the roads until those in the Churchill area.

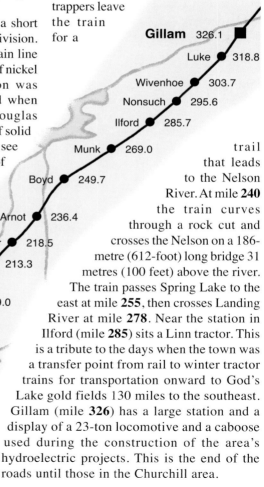

Gillam 326.1
Luke 318.8
Wivenhoe 303.7
Nonsuch 295.6
Ilford 285.7
Munk 269.0
Boyd 249.7
Arnot 236.4
Bridgar 218.5
Thompson 30.5
Pikwitonei 213.3
Grasbar 12.9
Thompson Jct 199.0
Leven 191.9
Thicket Portage 184.3
Hockin 177.6
La Perouse 171.1
164.3 Earchman
148.7 Lyddal
Wabowden 136.4

Route Highlights

Gillam to Churchill
Herchmer Subdivision

Miles 326–509: At mile **332** the largest bridge on the route, over 300 metres (1000 feet), crosses the Nelson River. To the west you can clearly see the Kettle generating station. Manitoba Hydro's second largest facility in the province, built from 1966 to 1973, is 885 metres (2900 feet) long, and contains 12 turbines. The train crosses the Limestone River at mile **349.8**. Watch to the east where the river flows into the Nelson, creating the Upper Limestone Rapids. At mile **351** to the east is the Limestone Generating Station.

Thus far, the route has actually been travelling toward Port Nelson, the site originally chosen for the line's northern terminus. In fact a 250-metre (2,460-foot) long bridge was built to cross the Nelson River, and the line was cleared and graded for track. It was then discov-

Thermal pipes along the route of the train.

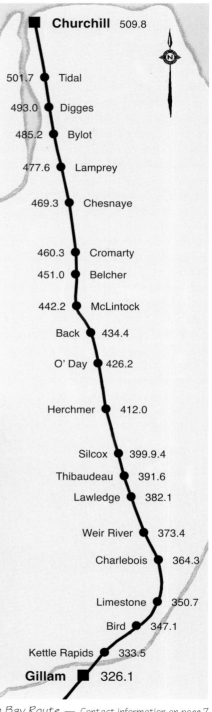

Churchill 509.8

501.7 Tidal

493.0 Digges

485.2 Bylot

477.6 Lamprey

469.3 Chesnaye

460.3 Cromarty

451.0 Belcher

442.2 McLintock

Back 434.4

O' Day 426.2

Herchmer 412.0

Silcox 399.9.4

Thibaudeau 391.6

Lawledge 382.1

Weir River 373.4

Charlebois 364.3

Limestone 350.7

Bird 347.1

Kettle Rapids 333.5

Gillam 326.1

ered that Port Nelson would not make an adequate port because of the silt deposits from the Nelson River. The decision was made to extend the line to Churchill; hence the sharp turn at mile **355**. Now the train travels through an area of stunted spruce and tamarack trees, with still more thermal pipes between miles **362** and **366**. The "communities" along the way are merely sidings named after local historical figures by the railway. The landscape is like no other you have passed since your trip began. Starting at mile **445** the train crosses the barren lands. The short trees grow to their leeward side, away from the predominant north winds. At mile **493** the red building on the east side of the tracks was once a telemetry station for the Churchill rocket range. Churchill comes into view at mile **507**, and you arrive at VIA's northernmost station at mile **509.8**. Look to the north to see the 140,000-tonne capacity grain elevator next to the mouth of the Churchill River.

The sights you see during a visit to Churchill vary by the season. In the winter months, you can witness the dancing northern lights; in the spring, birders come to glimpse the rare ross gull and other northern birds; the beluga whales appear in the summer months; and in the fall the famous polar bears are waiting for the ice to freeze on the bay. Attractions include the Eskimo Museum, Wapusk National Park, and the impressive town complex. While here, book a beluga whale tour by contacting Sea North Tours at: 888-348-7951. Call Frontiers North Adventures at: 800-663-9832 to book a trip on the world-famous Tundra Buggy. We also recommend you contact the Churchill Chamber of Commerce at: 888-389-2327, for information on available accommodations. To book an overview tour of the Churchill area, before you arrive, call Nature 1st at: 204-675-2147.

Churchill, Manitoba, is VIA Rail's most northern destination and the furthest north you can travel on continuouus trackage in North America.

The Skeena Route

One of the most picturesque rail journeys in the country, VIA Rail's *Skeena* takes passengers on a journey through the heart of British Columbia. Along the way, the passing scenery includes everything from mountains, meandering and rushing rivers, or glaciers, to areas where history appears to stand still. *The Skeena* runs year-round, with an overnight stop in Prince George.

Grand Trunk Pacific president Charles Melville Hays chose the community of Prince Rupert (then known as Port Simpson) for the western terminus of Canada's third transcontinental railway, which was built between 1911 and 1914. Hays never witnessed its completion, having been a passenger on the *Titanic*. Hays's vision continues today as *Canadian National* continues to operate freight trains over the line, while VIA operates the passenger train known locally as the "Rupert Rocket." Information about the first few miles of *The Skeena* route, and also the park town of Jasper with its great attractions and accommodations, are provided in the Jasper-to-Redpass portion of the *Canadian*, page 102.

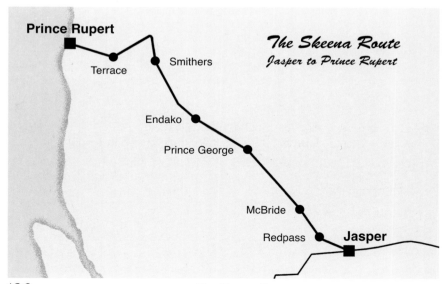

Low clouds hide the picturesque mountains at McBride, British Columbia.

Route Highlights
Red Pass Junction to Taverna
Robson Subdivision

Miles 0–20: At mile **2.4** the train crosses the Fraser River, which is followed by tracks on the north side of the route. To the south, the train travels along a rock cut; look up to get intermittent glimpses of the other railway tracks. Mount Robson, the highest peak in the Canadian Rockies at 3954 metres (12,972 feet) above sea level, continues to be seen to the north for the next few miles. The train crosses numerous mountain streams before arriving at Taverna, where the tracks turn south to Vancouver or west to McBride.

Route Highlights
Taverna to McBride
Tete Jaune Subdivision

Miles 0–43: The passing scenery includes everything from thick forests

and mountain streams to grazing cattle. Tete Jaune (Yellowhead) at mile **4.3** is named for the trapper and guide who led traders and explorers through the pass in the Rocky Mountains. It was also a stop for the sternwheelers that worked along the Fraser River. At mile **9.5** you cross the Little Shuswap River. The station in Dunster (mile **23.4**) is now a museum. At mile **25** you get a good view to the north over the meandering Fraser River; watch for bears and moose along the shores. River crossings continue with the Raush River Viaduct at mile **32** and Cottonwood Creek at mile **35**. The Eddy Creek Bridge at mile **39** is a good place to photograph your train. McBride, at mile **43**, is situated in the valley between the Rocky Mountains to the south and the Cariboo Mountains to the north. You pass the refurbished McBride Hotel before arriving at the 1919 station, which today serves as the McBride Arts Centre and as a Tourism Information Centre.

Route Highlights

McBride to Prince George
Fraser Subdivision.

Miles 0–69: The Fifty Mile River is crossed three times at miles **2.5, 6.4,**

56 was built in 1913, it halted all riverboat traffic on the Upper Fraser. The tracks now run along the north side of the river. Watch for the small Penny Post Office building in Penny, BC, at mile **69** on the south side of the tracks; its proportions are comparable to the village's size. The Penny Station was moved from this location to the Prince George Railway and Forest Museum here in 1986.

Miles **70–146:** At mile **70** the track straightens out and travels through a thickly forested area of spruce, hemlock, and

Prince George 146.0 — Shelley — Wolverina 136.3 — 123.6 — Giscome 122.4 — Lake 108.8 — Aleza — 100.2 — Hansard — Dewey 92.2 — Hutton 87.4 — Longworth 79.4 — Penny 69.5 — Guilford 65.0 — Bend 57.7 — Kidd 51.9 — Urling 45.1 — Loos 36.9 — 27.8 — Goat River — Poser 14.4 — McBride 43.4/0.0 — Raush Valley — Dunster 31.0 — Croydon 17.2

and **6.6.** The Skeena travels high above Twin Creek at mile **16.5** and at mile **18** enters a 250-metre (820-foot) tunnel. On the west side of the tunnel, the train travels along a stretch of track known for mud slides and falling rocks. At mile **25,** as the train skirts the Fraser River, you can see that the river has become much wider, as a result of the many creeks and tributaries feeding into it. A former sawmill, with its metal roof and weather-beaten walls, still stands on the south side of the tracks at mile **33.** The train crosses the meandering Snowshoe Creek at mile **38** and Catfish Creek at mile **40.** Ptarmigan Creek is first crossed at mile **46,** then again at mile **47;** the route follows the creek before it turns toward the Fraser. When the low bridge at mile

cedar. The train then makes several water crossings: Read Creek at mile **78,** Boulder Creek at mile **83,** Pritchard Creek at mile **91,** Cabin Creek at mile **93.2,** and Ringland Creek at mile **93.7.** The most interesting river crossing is at mile **99** where *The Skeena* again traverses the Fraser; since vehicles also use this 295-metre (968-foot) long bridge to cross the river, you might see a long line of motorists waiting for your train to get across. Upper Fraser, at mile **104**, is a company town for the large lumber mill that can be seen to the north. Also to the north, between miles **105** and **108**, you can see Hansard and Aleza lakes. Eaglet Lake can also be seen on the north side of the tracks at miles **117** and **121**. Giscome, at mile **122**, features a large gravel quarry; much of the rock quarried here is used for railway ballast in western Canada. The General Store at Willow River is still operating at mile **127**. The Fraser River comes into view again to the north. On the opposite shore at mile **136**, Simon Fraser established the North West Company's Fort George trading post in 1807. At mile **143**, *The Skeena* travels under the British Columbia Railway trestle across the Fraser River. The Skeena makes its own river crossing on the Grand Trunk Bridge, starting at mile **144.7**; the Yellowhead Highway Bridge can be seen to the west. You pass the mile **145**

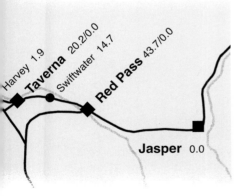

marker on the bridge near the opposite shore. After crossing this wide river, you pass through the CN Prince George rail yards and arrive at the station at mile **146**.

Known as BC's "Northern Capital," Prince George has no shortage of things to do or see. As *The Skeena* lays over here for the night, you might get a chance to walk around the downtown area and visit its numerous boutiques, or enjoy the colourful nightlife. We recommend you book your hotel reservations well in advance of your visit. One hotel to consider is the Ramada, located at 444 George Street. You can make reservations at: 250-563-0055. Web: *www.ramadaprincegeorge.com*. Also highly recommended is the Prince George Railway and Forest Museum, which offers a great way to learn more about the history of the railway and the forest industry in this region. Displays at the museum, located near Cottonwood Island Park and close to the CN rail yards, include a wooden 1903 Russell snowplow, and an 8-foot diameter band saw once used in Giscome. The museum is open daily from May until September. Groups travelling by train are encouraged to contact them in advance for group tours at: 250-563-7351. Web: *www.pgrfm.bc.ca*

If you are planning a visit to Prince George, contact Tourism Prince George, 101 - 1300 First Avenue, Prince George, BC V2L 2Y3. Call: 800-668-7646 or visit: *www. tourism.pg.bc.ca*. If you plan to leave the train anywhere along the route of *The Skeena*, you can obtain information from the Northern British Columbia Tourism Association, Box 2373, Prince George, BC V2N 2S6. Call: 800-663-8843. Web: *www.northernbctravel.com*

Route Highlights

Prince George to Endako
Nechako Subdivision

Miles 0–30: As you move through the CN Prince George yards, look to the north to see the steep banks of the Nechako River. This is the site of the Sandblast event every August; contestants ski and snowboard down this sandy cutbank and are judged on best style and costumes. The train moves swiftly through Prince George, and the city is soon left behind. At mile **15** the Chilako River (which translates to "river of mud") is crossed. As mile **30** approaches, keep watching the river for the Isle de Pierre Rapids, a considerable navigation obstacle for the riverboats that once travelled up and down the river.

Miles 30–68: Fishermen are not the only ones who try to catch the Nechako's prize-winning trout. You might also catch a glimpse of an osprey swooping toward the river to catch lunch. The sandbank on the opposite shore of the river at mile **58** makes for an interesting photo. Between miles **63** and **68** the tracks form the southern border of the Nechako Migratory Bird Sanctuary, which is home to various types of birds, most notably migrating Canadian Geese.

Miles 68–92: Vanderhoof, named after a *Grand Trunk Pacific* advertising agent, is reached at mile **69**. Look to the south to see the Vanderhoof Heritage Museum. With its restored village, you can return to a farming community of the Nechako Valley in the 1920s. The museum also has a modern CN transfer caboose. *The Skeena* continues past large lumber mills and farmers' fields. Watch to the south at mile 89 to see an early homestead built in a V-shape, possibly to take advantage of the view.

Mile 93: The picnic table and roadside stop on the south side of the tracks overlook the spot where the last spike on the Grand Trunk Pacific was put in place on April 7, 1914. The honour of driving it home fell to the west crew construction foreman Peter Titiryn. It was declared a Heritage Site in 1998.

VIA Rail's *Skeena* crosses high above Boulder Creek.

The Skeena Route — Contact information on page 7

Miles **94–115**: At mile **94** the train passes through Fort Fraser. This community dates to 1806, when Simon Fraser started a trading centre called the Fraser Lake Post; it was a large community during the heyday of railway construction. At mile **95** *The Skeena* crosses the Nechako River. Then, between miles **100** and **108**, the picturesque Lake Fraser can be seen to the north. White Swan Park (mile **107**) is a popular picnic spot in the summer months. At mile **109.5** the train crosses the swift-moving Stellako River. Endako (mile **115**) is very unassuming as a divisional point, with only a few buildings along the highway. It does feature a modern bunkhouse for the CNR freight crews.

Route Highlights

Endako to Smithers
Telkwa Subdivision

Miles 0–55: At mile **10.9** *The Skeena* crosses the Endako River for the first time. This meandering river will be crossed a total of eight times between here and mile **21.7**. While you count the crossings, look at mile **15** to catch a glimpse of part of an old railway boxcar in the bush; this marks the spot of the former railway town of Freeport. Passing through the marsh at mile **19**, you might notice the log pylons along the north side of the tracks. These pylons were installed by a steam pile driver to stabilize the right of way. At mile **27**, on the north side of the tracks next to the highway, look for a stone cairn at a roadside stop. The cairn features a stone from the Tintagel Castle in Cornwall, England (thought by some historians to be the birthplace of King Arthur, known for forming the Knights of the Round

Table). At mile **32** Burns Lake comes into view. The fill used to cross a portion of the lake comes from the "Big Cut." This is where the railway contractors had the most difficulty building the line. Deadman's Island now sits quietly in the middle of the lake; however, it received its name for a horrific construction accident, when 15 men near the cut and another 15 standing on the island died in a blasting accident. The lake ends at mile **35** at the community of Burns Lake. This is a popular starting point for a visit to the Tweedsmuir Provincial Park, located to the south. Decker Lake can be seen to the south at miles **38** and **39**, and the train passes the lake at miles **53** through **55**. Situated on a watershed, Decker Lake empties to the east towards the Fraser River and to the west towards the Skeena. The Nadina and Pimpernel mountains sit on the opposite side of the lake.

Miles **56–125**: Starting at mile **56**, the train makes the first of 11 crossings of the Bulkley River; the last will be made at **84.3** as the train travels through the Bulkley River Valley. Houston (mile **85**) is renowned for its steelhead and coho salmon fishing. They must be big here—the largest fly fishing rod (18.3 metres/60 feet in length) can be seen in Steelhead Park on the south side of the tracks, as well as a steelhead sculpture. At mile **93** *The Skeena* crosses the Morice River. Keep your camera pointed to the south at mile **98** for a view of the Telkwa Mountains, obscured slightly by a unique 830-metre (2,725-foot) high round hill in the foreground. Mile **103** brings you to a good curve to photograph your train. Turn your camera to the north at mile **104** and look across the Bulkley River for your first views of the Skeena Mountain Range.

Where you cross the Telkwa River, look to the north to see the town of Telkwa where the river empties into the Bulkley River. On the south side of the bridge you can see the pilings of a former river crossing. At mile **125** you arrive at the large Smithers Station, built in 1918. Since this station was built by *Grand Trunk Pacific* as part of its Winnipeg-to-Prince Rupert line, the station sign proudly proclaims the distance in miles between these two points. The eastern portion of the line, the *National Transcontinental Railway*, was built by the federal government and

Route Highlights

Smithers to Terrace
Bulkley Subdivision

Miles 0–19: The square-looking building directly behind the station is the Smithers Centennial Library. Beside that is the Veterans' Peace Park, with a *Canadian National Railways* flanger. This piece of equipment used its blades below it to remove the snow between the rails. Kathlyn Lake, to the south between miles **3** and **4**, was renamed by the railway for use in its advertising. It

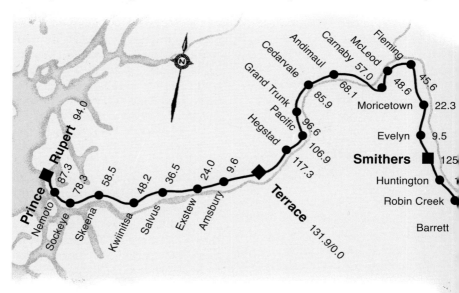

stretched from Winnipeg to Moncton, New Brunswick. The plan was for it to be operated by the GTP, but when the line was completed, the GTP could not make the required payments to the government. Thus it became incorporated into the government-owned *Canadian National Railway*.

If your train is on time, you might get a chance to stretch your legs here on the platform and visit the station.

was originally known to the First Nations people as Chicken Lake. In the background above the lake, you get some fine views of the Kathlyn Glacier atop Hudson Bay Mountain. Toboggan Creek is crossed at miles **7.7** and **8.3**. The Toboggan Creek hatchery, on the north side of the tracks at mile **9**, researches the management of the coho and steelhead stocks in the upper Skeena watershed. At the hatchery, they tag these fish, collecting data on their life cycle when the fish return to spawn. *The Skeena* crosses the Trout Creek Viaduct at mile **13** and then enters a 121-metre (400-foot) tunnel. At mile **19** the train crosses John Brown Creek and travels past Wet'sewet'en First Nations reserve at Moricetown.

Miles **20–44**: At mile **22** look to the south for views of Brian Boru and Tiltusha peaks. Keep your camera ready for the spectacular view from the Boulder Creek Bridge at mile **28.4**; the bridge curves to the north, offering a great opportunity to photograph your train. At mile **31** you cross Porphyry Creek, with commanding views to the north of Mount Seaton and Blunt Mountain. The views continue at the Mud Creek trestle, with Hagwilget Peak to the south. Look down to the river below to see glimpses of its white water at mile **40.8**; you then immediately enter the longest CN tunnel that a passenger train travels through, at 629 metres (2065 feet).

The train passes through two more tunnels at miles **41.9** and **43.3**.

Miles **44–84**: *The Skeena* reaches New Hazelton at mile **45**. Located at the base of Rocher Deboule, the town was named for the abundance of hazelnuts in the area. The community dates to 1866 when it was a Hudson Bay trading post; later it was a stop for the steamboats serving the isolated communities along the Skeena River. As the train crosses the Sealy Gulch Bridge at mile **50**, look to the north to see the mountains of the Kispiox Mountain Range. Passing the impressive green rolling mountains, the train crosses the Skeena River at mile **62**. The community of Kitseguecla can be seen on the north side of the river. (Try and get your fellow passengers to repeat that name three times!) Kitwanga at mile **73** has been inhabited by the Gitksan First Nations people for hundreds of years. Keep your camera pointed to the south to photograph one of the community's totem poles; then the train passes through the middle of the village's cemetery. Look to the south as the train crosses Highway 37 to catch a glimpse of the former railway station and the 1893 St. Paul's Anglican Church. The train passes through another tunnel at mile **78**. A native smokehouse on the river bank is passed at mile **83**.

79.0

66.5

57.5

45.4

35.0

27.4

6.6

115.4/0.0

102.0

90.8

82.6

69.4

66.3

45.7

27.8

7.2

0.0

ropley

Broman Lake

Palling

Burns Lake

Tintagel

Savory

Endako

Encombe

Willowvale

Engen

Vanderhoof

Cariboo

Wedgwood

Nichol

Nechako

Prince

George

Miles **85–131:** The venerable Mrs. Essex is now gone, but the Cedarvale general store and post office is still standing. It can be seen among the trees on the south side of the tracks at mile **86.3**. Mrs. Essex, Canada's longest-serving post mistress, worked here for 73 years from 1923 to 1996. At mile **90** you pass through another tunnel, and then cross Porcupine Creek at mile **93**. There are good views to the north and south as you move along the river. Just a few buildings are left along a grassy trail in Doreen (mile **100**), a town that has survived far better than Pacific at mile **106.9**. Once a thriving railway community when steam locomotives served the region, all that remains of Pacific is a stone fireplace, a few foundations, and a forlorn class 1 station rebuilt from a boxcar. At mile **119** watch for the red and white poles used by the vehicle ferry in Usk. The ferry is propelled by the river's swift current and by large blades located underneath the ferry. The tracks move away from the river to pass through a quartet of tunnels located at miles **121.9**, **122.1**, **122.3**, and **122.8**. The bridge for the Kitimat subdivision that crosses the river can be seen at mile **130**. Terrace is reached at mile **131.9**.

Route Highlights

Terrace to Prince Rupert
Bulkley Subdivision

Miles 0–44: The last stretch through the Coastal Mountains offers some of the most spectacular sights of the entire trip. The river becomes wider as the train approaches the Pacific Ocean. In the summer months, it is quite common to see fishermen along the shore trying to catch a prize-winning salmon. The Kitsumkaylus River is crossed at mile **3.1** and the Zimacord River at mile **7.3**. At times the train moves away from the river, but you still get excellent views of the Kitimat Mountain Range to the south. Watch for bears along the shoreline; you may even catch a glimpse of the rare white Kermode bear. Also, watch the river for playful seals bobbing with the current and, above the train, for circling eagles. At mile **34** the train crosses the Ex-Chom-Siks River. While crossing the Ka-Its-Siks River at mile **39**, look up towards the cliff to see one of the many waterfalls. These cascading waterfalls are most common in the spring, when the snow from the mountains is melting. During the Second World War, this rail line was exceptionally busy, shipping supplies to Prince Rupert destined for Alaska and carrying troops destined for overseas. At that time, it was feared that Japanese fishermen who knew the river well from pre-war days could give detailed information to the Japanese Navy; such information might then have been used to plan commando raids to blow up a railway bridge or tunnel. The Canadian Government and the CNR built Canada's No. 1 Armoured Train in Winnipeg to protect the vital rail link. It featured gondola cars with a 75-mm gun on each end, 40-mm anti-aircraft guns, modified boxcars with 15-mm armoured plating, and a locomotive in the middle to move the train. Since it never saw combat, the train was relegated to training trips near the end of the war, with strict instructions to gunners NOT to damage private property.

Miles **45–96:** Mile **48** was once the site of the Kwinitsa Station. In 1985 the station was barged down the Skeena River to Prince Rupert and preserved on the city's waterfront. The Ky-Ax River is crossed at mile **60**. At mile **67** look to the

A BC Ferry docked at Prince Rupert and ready to depart.

rocks on the north side of the tracks to see some recently uncovered First Nations pictographs. Next to the river you can see the large log pilings in the river; they are all that remain of a salmon cannery after the buildings were removed due to losses. At mile **80** look to the west down the Skeena River for a fantastic view where the river empties into the Pacific Ocean. At mile **81** you pass the North Pacific Fishing Village; this former cannery, built in 1889, was recognized as a National Historic Site in 1996. It features guided tours, a restaurant, and overnight accommodation. In the 1920s, Icelandic settlers from the Gimli, Manitoba, area settled the now-abandoned town of Osland, on Smith Island at mile **83**. From mile **84** to **87** Lelu and Ridley Island can be seen in Chatham Sound. At mile **87** the train passes a large grain terminal and crosses a bridge over the Zanardi Rapids (located in the Wainwright Basin) and onto Kaien Island. Where the train skirts the Pacific Ocean, watch the shoreline along the tracks for the large concrete platform from which searchlights watched the harbour during the Second World War. The BC and Alaska Ferry Terminals come into view at mile **92**, near the end of your journey.

Although he never lived to see the railway reach the port town he envisioned, a statue of Charles Melville Hays stands proudly beside the Prince Rupert City Hall. Whether you have come to visit for wildlife, history, or a fishing adventure, you will find no shortage of things to do. We highly recommend a visit to the Museum of Northern British Columbia, where you can learn more about the Haida First Nations people and their ancient culture. After your museum visit, stroll through Mariners' Memorial Park, dedicated to those who never returned to port. Further on, you come to Cow Bay, with its shops and cafés on Prince Rupert's waterfront. The Fire Hall Museum, with its local law enforcement and fire fighter history, as well as a 1925 REO Speedwagon fire engine, is very interesting. To learn more about the rail trip you took to get here, and the area's rail heritage, do not miss the Kwinitsa Station Museum.

After your journey on the rails, we recommend the Pacific Inn, located at 909 Third Avenue West. Reservations can be made by calling them at: 888-663-1999.

For more information and to plan your visit in advance, we recommend you contact the Prince Rupert Visitor Info Centre at PO Box 669, Prince Rupert, BC V8J 3S1. Call: 800-667-1994. Web: *www.tourismprincerupert.com*

Malahat Dayliner

In **1884** the *Esquimalt and Nanaimo Railway* was incorporated by the *Canadian Pacific Railway* to connect to the rest of the transcontinental system and the BC provincial capital of Victoria (located on Vancouver Island). The line was planned to connect from Esquimalt, a suburb of Victoria, to the northern island community of Nanaimo, where passengers could transfer to a ferry that travelled to Vancouver. One of the railway's prime movers was industrialist Robert Dunsmuir, who envisioned that the presence of the railway would increase the value of his holdings in the island's interior.

Victoria, one of the oldest European settlements in the area, features an Old World flavour in a modern cosmopolitan city. Attractions include the Provincial Legislature, the Royal British Columbia Museum, a whale-watching tour, ghost walks as the sun sets, and Miniature World, where in no time at all you can watch a train travel from the Atlantic to the Pacific.

As you will need more than a few days to take in the city's sights, we recommend you stay at the Empress Hotel. Conveniently located near the bus depot and a short distance from the railway station at 721 Government Road, this grand old railway hotel still serves afternoon tea in the lobby overlooking the Inner Harbour, a tradition that dates from the hotel's opening in 1908. Reservations can be made at: 800-441-1414. Web: *www.fairmont.com*. The journey begins from Victoria's station at 450 Pandora Avenue.

VIA Rail's *Malahat* at Victoria, BC, before its morning departure.

Malahat Dayliner — Contact information on page 7

Route Highlights

Victoria to Courtney
Victoria Subdivision

Miles 0–72: Once your train is past the quaint brick Victoria station, it crosses the Johnson Street interlocking bridge— look to the west for a view of the Inner Harbour. At mile **1**, watch to the east side of the tracks to see the historic brick railway roundhouse and shops. The train then moves through an industrial and housing area built around the Esquimalt Naval Base. At mile **3** keep watching to the west; you might see some of the Canadian Navy's Pacific Fleet moored at Esquimalt's large docks. Also watch for the salmon smokehouses of the Esquimalt First Nations reserve. The Fort Victoria RV Park, with an interesting replica of a fortification, is passed at mile **4**. The train passes Langford, a bedroom community of Victoria. At mile **9**, Langford Lake can be seen to the east. At mile **11.5** the train crosses an underground pipe that supplies water to the Greater Victoria area. At mile **11.8** the train crosses Goldstream River, enters Goldstream Provincial Park, and starts climbing Malahat Mountain. You cross the Niagara Canyon on a cantilever bridge at mile **14**, and then the Arbutus Canyon at mile **14.9**—look to the east to see the Finlayson Arm of the Squally Reach. At mile **16** the Malahat passes through the only tunnel on the line. At mile **20** you reach Malahat's Summit. At mile **25** a small stone cairn marks the spot where, on August 13, 1886, Canada's first prime minister, Sir John A. MacDonald, drove the last spike on the E&N. Lake Shawnigan is seen to the west between miles **26** and **28**.

The 1912 station in Duncan (mile **39**), with a preserved caboose, is now the Cowichan Valley Museum. The scenery changes as the train travels through the agricultural areas of the Westholme Valley. The Chemainus River is crossed at mile **47**; at mile **50** watch to the east to see a preserved MacMillan & Bloedel logging locomotive. Chemainus (mile **52.1**) is known for its historical murals. It has a preserved caboose for a station. Located in a region once known for numerous coaling operations, Ladysmith

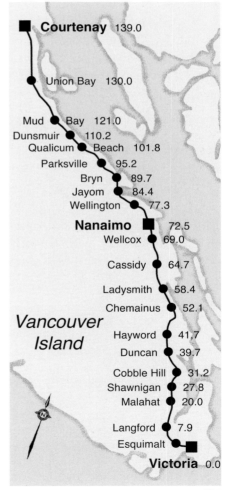

■ **Courtenay** 139.0

● Union Bay 130.0

Mud ● Bay 121.0
Dunsmuir ● 110.2
Qualicum ● Beach 101.8
Parksville ● 95.2
Bryn ● 89.7
Jayom ● 84.4
Wellington ● 77.3
Nanaimo ■ 72.5
Wellcox ● 69.0

Cassidy ● 64.7

Ladysmith ● 58.4
Chemainus ● 52.1

Vancouver Island

Hayword ● 41.7
Duncan ● 39.7

Cobble Hill ● 31.2
Shawnigan ● 27.8
Malahat ● 20.0

Langford ● 7.9
Esquimalt ■
Victoria 0.0

The *Malahat Dayliner* at the end of the line, Courtenay, BC, awaiting departure for the return trip to Victoria.

is at mile **58**. To the east is beautiful Transfer Park, which hosts the popular Dogwood Days during the last weekend of August. Coal Creek is crossed at mile **60**. The *Malahat Dayliner* is the only train in Canada where you can witness someone bungee jumping. At mile **65**, where the train crosses the Nanaimo River, look to the west to see the bridge where the thrill-seekers leap. Nanaimo's station is reached at mile **72.5**.

Miles **73–139:** This line was purchased by the *Canadian Pacific Railway* in 1905, and extended north to reach Courtenay in 1914. At mile **74**, look to the east to see the large BC Ferry terminal where ferries connect with the Horseshoe Bay terminal and the mainland. Nanoose Bay, with its naval base on the opposite shore, can be seen between miles **83** and **86**. The train crosses the Englishman River at mile **93**. Parksville (mile **95**) offers a rare sight in the 21st century, a heritage railway station and water tower. The track that continues to the west goes to Port Alberni, where you can view the McLean Mill National Historic Site and ride behind a restored logging train. The

Malahat Dayliner crosses French Creek at mile **99** on a 318-metre (1,045-foot) long trestle—the longest on the line. Another former logging locomotive, Bloedel Stewart & Welch No. 4, can be seen to the east at mile **101** before you arrive at the Qualicum Beach station. One of the province's many salmon hatcheries is located on the Big Qualicum River, crossed at mile **110**; keep watching to the east for a view of the Strait of Georgia. Meandering Cook Creek lives up to its name—the train crosses it four times at mile **119**. Mud Bay can be seen to the east at mile **121**. When you cross the T'Sable River at mile **125**, look to the east for views of Denman Island. At mile **126** you see the BC ferry terminal that provides service to the island from Buckley Bay. Between miles **128** and **129** more great views are offered to the east, this time of Union Bay. At mile **137** Courtenay's sister city, Comox, appears in the distance. The *Malahat Dayliner* arrives at the historic Courtenay Station at mile **139,** and prepares for the return journey. It is quite common for a snack truck to meet the train, offering sandwiches or ice cream treats.

Malahat Dayliner — Contact information on page 7

The Excursions

With Canada's rich history of rail travel, almost every corner of Canada features an enjoyable rail excursion that can be enjoyed by young and old. These excursion trips are spread across the country from Nova Scotia to British Columbia and include everything from an afternoon trip to a local flea market in Ontario to a several-days tour in southern Alberta aboard a restored business car once used by Sir Winston Churchill!

Many of the excursions are operated by the volunteers of preservation groups who believe strongly in sharing their passion and wish the next generation to experience the traditions of the past. The hard work of these organizations and their volunteers should not go unnoticed and unappreciated. The loving touches can be seen in everything they organize, from the period costumes they wear to the restoration of the equipment used. As well, tour companies operate rail excursions that feature outstanding scenery, and tell the stories of communities no longer served by regularly-scheduled passenger trains.

As schedules and frequencies are subject to change, we highly recommend that before you go, you research the location of the excursions, costs, and departure times. Don't hesitate to ask staff and volunteers about other displays that are associated with the excursions, or attractions and accommodations in the communities where they serve. The following selections do not encompass *every* excursion in Canada, many of which are operated at our country's railway museums. To learn more about each province's rail excursions we recommend you contact the provincial tourism organizations listed throughout this guide.

The Bras d'Or

Nova Scotia is known for its outstanding scenery, and one of the best ways to view it is from VIA Rail's *Bras d'Or*, which departs Halifax during the summer and fall months for a day trip to Sydney on beautiful Cape Breton Island. Return trip is the following day. For more information on departures and availability, please contact VIA Rail at: 888-842-7245. Web: *www.viarail.ca*

The train travels from Halifax on the Bedford Subdivision (following the route of VIA's *Ocean*, which is detailed on page 14) before turning north at Truro.

Route Highlights

Truro to Havre Boucher
Hopewell Subdivision

Miles 0–116: A switch is thrown and the train turns north, away from Truro and the *Canadian National* east-west mainline, onto the tracks operated by the *Cape Breton and Central Nova Scotia Railway*. Between miles **3** and **17** the train travels through the lush Salmon River Valley, reaching the Gordon Summit at mile **23**. Look for views of the valley to the west at mile **28**. At mile **40** the train enters the railway yards in Stellarton. Look to the west at mile **41** to see the Nova Scotia Museum of Industry building which houses the oldest railway locomotive in Canada, as well as other displays related to this coal mining region. At mile **42** the train crosses the East River and enters New Glasgow. After passing the ornate post office building, to the east, look for the former general store that the railway purchased because it was in the way. It was divided into two parts (with a connecting tunnel underneath) to allow the

tracks to continue! At mile **51** you see Pictou Harbour to the west. The train crosses Barney River twice, first at mile **65.9** and again at mile **66.1**. At mile **84** the train passes the Antigonish Heritage Museum, housed in the community's 1908 *Intercolonial Railway* station.

Good views of the southern portion of Antigonish Harbour can be seen to the west between miles **85** and **88**. The train returns to a forested area. Tracadie Bay can be seen to the west between miles **103** and **106**. Then great views over St. Georges Bay begin at mile **113**. The train arrives at Havre Boucher at mile **116**.

Route Highlights

Havre Boucher to Sydney
Sydney Subdivision

Miles 0–112: Good views can be seen to the north as the Strait of Canso and Cape Breton Island

pleted in 1955. A swing bridge is located at mile **8.7**, above a lock system that permits boats to pass. The train reaches Port Hawkesbury at mile **12.3**. The Orangedale Railway Museum at mile **41** is located in and around the community's *Intercolonial Railway* station. Keep your camera ready at mile **47** for the curved trestle over the Ottawa Brook. At mile **53** the train emerges from the forest. Canada's largest inland sea, the Bras d'Or Lake, comes into view to the east. This area is known for sighting eagles over the lake's white cliffs. At mile **57** the train

Gannon 92.6
Jefferson 108.1
Sydney 113.9

Georges
Boisdale
Cross
River
92.8
Point 71.9
McKinnon
Grand
Narrows 52.1
58.1
Orangedale
River Denys
41.2
Harbour
33.2
Antigonish
Port Hawkesbury
Havre
Afton
84.2
100.1
Boucher 116/0.0
12.3
Hope 70.8
,COTIA

come into view. The train crosses the Strait at mile **8** on the Canso Causeway which connects the Nova Scotia mainland and Cape Breton Island. Rock from Cape Porcupine (seen to the east) was used to build this causeway, which was com-

reaches Iona. You can see the Saint Columbia Presbyterian Church to the west before you cross the 517-metre (1,697-foot) long Grand Narrows Bridge. Once across look to the east to see the Grand Narrows Hotel; visitors to this modest lodging have included Governor General Lord Stanley (who opened the bridge in 1897), Alexander Graham Bell, Helen Keller, the Wright Brothers, and Canadian prime ministers Sir John A. Macdonald and Sir Charles Tupper. The lake is now to the west of the train; at mile **60** you pass Christmas Island, named after the Micmac Chief Noel who is buried there. The train continues to move along the lake, and views over what is known as St. Andrews channel continue between miles **67** and **84**. At mile **87** the train crosses a 105-metre (346-foot) long bridge over George's River. At mile **95** the train

Orangedale Station is now a museum along the route of the Bras D'or.

crosses a causeway that offers good views of the Atlantic Ocean to the north. This is the northernmost part of your trip; you might be able to see one of the large ferries that travel between North Sydney and Newfoundland. The former station with a caboose in

Sydney Mines lives on as an ice cream parlour. North Sydney (mile **98**) has two stations—the one next to the tracks, and the original station, which now houses the offices of the John C. MacKinnon Lumber yard. Sydney Harbour comes into view before you arrive at the platform for Sydney at mile **113.9**. After a long day's journey, we recommend the Delta Sydney located at 300 Esplanade. Reservations can be made by contacting them at: 800-268-1133, or at: 902-562-7500.

No longer just a coal mining area, Sydney has many attractions and is a great place to start your exploration of the region. After spending a few days in the city, you may want to head north to the beautiful Cabot Trail and the Cape Breton Highlands National Park. Or go southeast to the Cape Breton Miners Museum and Village in Glace Bay to learn more about this coal-rich region and how it was once mined. Further along the highway, you will arrive at Louisbourg, home to the Louisbourg Railway Museum, and the recreated Fortress of Louisbourg National Historic Site. Tours and sightseeing for visitors can be organized through Sydney and Louisbourg Railway Museum, PO Box 35, Louisbourg, NS B0A 1M7. Call: 902-733-2767.

Evangeline Express

One of the most enjoyable ways to travel near the shores of the Minas Basin, on Nova Scotia's Bay of Fundy in the eastern Annapolis Valley, is on the open-air cars of the Windor and Hantsport Railway's *Evangeline Express*. On Sundays during the summer months there are two departures from Windsor to Wolfville and return. Windsor is located only 40 minutes from Halifax, NS. Travel on Highway 101, taking exit 6 towards Windsor. For more information on departures or advance tickets, we recommend you call: 902-798-5667.

Route Highlights

Windsor to Wolfville
Halifax Subdivision

Miles 31–49: After departing, the train crosses a 914-metre (3,000-foot) long causeway over the Avon River. Hantsport station, built in 1919, can be seen to the east at mile **38.1**. At mile **44** the sweeping curve offers good views to both sides before the train crosses the Gaspereau River. At mile **45** you can see the three-metre (10-foot) high black Embarkation Cross; it was erected in 1924 in memory of the Acadians (descendants of French settlers) who were deported from the area in 1755. Grand Pre, passed at mile **46**, was established in 1907 when an individual purchased land that is believed to be the site of an Acadian village. The land was later sold to the *Dominion Atlantic Railway* on the condition that the Acadian people be involved with its upkeep. In 1920 the railway erected a statue of "Evangeline," the heroine in Henry Wadsworth Longfellow's poem about the plight of the Acadians. The statue can be seen near the tracks; inside the memorial church behind the statue are large murals that tell the story of the expulsion. The park became a National Historic Site in 1961. The train travels past an area once farmed by the Acadians, before arriving at the Wolfville Station, now the town's library, at mile **49**. Take some time to stroll around the Main Street of this community (which is home to Acadia University) before you reboard your train for the return trip.

The *Evangeline Express* at Windsor getting ready for its Sunday departure.

Salem and Hillsborough

*L*ocated in the heart of New Brunswick, 25 kilometres south of the city of Moncton, the *Salem and Hillsborough Railroad* features one of the best collections of railway equipment and artifacts in the province. Visitors are encouraged to visit the museum before boarding the excursion trains that are operated on Sundays from mid-June to Labour Day, and on Wednesdays and some Saturdays from mid-July to mid-August. For more information about departure schedules or advance tickets, we recommend you contact the *Salem and Hillsborough Railroad*, 2847 Main Street, Hillsborough, NB E4H 2X7. Call: 506-734-3195. Web: *www.go.to/shrailroad*

Route Highlights

Hillsborough to Salem Station
Hillsborough Subdivision

Miles 24–19: Departing Hillsborough, look to the west to see the family home of William H Steeves, a Father of Confederation, that has been restored to its 1850s appearance and houses the local museum. Opposite the Steeves family home up above sits St. Mary's Anglican Church, completed in 1896. For over 100 years the Albert Manufacturing Company mined and produced products from the area's gypsum. Look to the west on the shores of the Petticodiac River to see two large concrete silos that once stored gypsum before it was transferred to marine vessels. The fields on the east side of the train were once part of the river, but were reclaimed by the Acadian people for farming and grazing lands. At mile **23.2** the train crosses Grays Island Road; on the opposite shore of the Petitcodiac River you see the community of Pre-den-haut and the Notre-Dame-de-l'Annonciation church. At mile **21.9** the train crosses the Weldon Creek Bridge; Weldon Creek is subject to the Bay of Fundy's world famous tides—depending on the time of day you are crossing the river, tides can be anywhere from 30 centimetres to 9 metres (1 foot to 30 feet) deep! Dawson Road is crossed at mile **21.2**, then the train passes the large T.P. Downy sawmill and logging operation. At mile **20.7**, the curved Hiram Trestle is a great place to photograph your train. At over 63-metres (209-feet) long and 13-metres (44-feet) high, it is one of the largest wooden railway trestles still in use in New Brunswick. After moving through a forested area, the excursion train reaches a small section house at mile **19.8**, marking Salem. Passengers are welcome to stretch their legs while the locomotive is shunted to the opposite end of the train for the return trip. Dinner trains continue past this point to Baltimore at mile **13.7**, featuring such highlights as Oil Hill in the distance, and beautiful woodland vegetation best seen seen during the fall season when the trees are ablaze with colours.

138

Chaudiere Appalachian

*J*ncorporated in 1875, the *Quebec Central Railway* served the region from Levis, on the south shore of the St. Lawrence River, along the Chaudiere River Valley to Sherbrooke. Much of the line, a division of the *Canadian Pacific Railway*, was abandoned in the years up to 1994. Fortunately, most of the rails were left in place so, with its rebirth, passengers can once again enjoy the scenery of Quebec's Beauce Region while riding aboard the *Chaudiere Appalachian*. Trains operate from May to October. For more information, contact Chaudiere-Appalachian Tourist Trains, 399 J.M. Rosseau Blvd., PO Box 639, Vallee-Jonction, QC G0S 3J0. Call: 877-642-5580. Web: *http://beaucerail.iquebec.com*

Since the line uses two different subdivisions (the Vallee Subdivision and the Chaudiere Subdivision), trips may vary. Detailed here is the trip from Vallee Jonction to East Broughton with mileage that works in reverse.

Route Highlights

Vallee Jonction to East Broughton
Vallee Subdivision

Miles 0–85: All trips begin at the Vallee Jonction station at mile **0** of the Chaudiere Subdivision. Before you depart, visit the museum dedicated to the history of the *Quebec Central Railway*. From here the train switches to the Vallee Jonction Subdivision and crosses the Chaudiere River on a 158-metre (520-foot) long bridge, offering good views to both sides. These views over the valley continue to the east at miles **95** and **96**. The train continues past farms and forests near St. Frederick. At mile **90.3** the train passes Tring Junction with

its historic station. This is where tracks once travelled south to Lake Megantic. Summit (mile **87.2**) is the highest point on the route, and is where the train passes the offices for Express Marco Trucking and the offices for the new *Quebec Central Railway* shortline. East Broughton is reached at mile **85**, where passengers can stretch their legs before the return trip to Vallee Jonction.

Scenic journey in southern Quebec — *C&A Tourist Train photo*

Hull-Chelsea-Wakefield

Built in 1889 by the *Ottawa and Gatineau Valley Railway*, this line's excursion aboard the *Hull-Chelsea-Wakefield Steam Train* provides onboard entertainers and guides for the enjoyment of its passengers. Using a 1907 Swedish steam locomotive and European passenger cars, the train travels through the scenic Outaouais region along the Gatineau River to Wakefield, Quebec. The train operates from May to mid-October with the fall foliage season being the most popular time to take the trip. There are two different types of trips — a one-day excursion, and a Sunset Dinner Train, featuring fine cuisine. The trains depart from Hull, the sister city of Canada's capital, Ottawa, at 165 Rue Deveault. For more information contact the Hull-Chelsea-Wakefield Steam Train, 165 Rue Deveault, Hull, QC J8Z 1S7. Call: 800-871-7246. Web: *www.steamtrain.ca*

Route Highlights

Hull to Wakefield

Miles 0–85: After departing Hull, the train reaches Laman at mile **1.4** where the tracks of the Lachute Subdivision of the *Quebec-Gatineau Railway* are crossed. Then the train climbs the terraced rock formations of what is known as Mile Hill. At mile **6.5** the train passes through the community of Chelsea. Farm Point is passed at mile **17**. Keep watching to the east to spot the red Gendron covered bridge that was rebuilt in 1997 after being destroyed by fire. A former *Canadian Pacific Railway* station, built in 1927 and now housing the Pot au Feu restaurant, is reached at mile **19.7**.

Visitors will have time to stretch their legs in Wakefield and explore the attractions of the picturesque village. Attractions include the Maclaren Grist Mill that dates back to 1838, as well as a pioneer cemetery where former Canadian Prime Minister Lester B. Pearson is buried. If you get back to the station in time, before boarding the train for the trip back to Hull, you can see the locomotive being turned on a turntable by hand!

Fall colours in the Ottawa Valley. — *HCW Steam Train photo*

Hull-Chelsea-Wakefield Steam Train — Contact information on page 140

London and Port Stanley

*O*perating on a portion of the former *London and Port Stanley Railway* that connected Port Stanley with St. Thomas, ON, today the *London and Port Stanley Terminal Railway* takes passengers on a scenic 11-kilometre (7-mile) excursion. The train departs from the Port Stanley Station year-round on Sundays; on Saturdays between May to November; and daily from July 1 to Labour Day. For more information, contact Port Stanley Terminal Railway, 309 Bridge St., Port Stanley, ON N5L 1C5. Call: 877-244-4478. Web: *www.pstr.on.ca*. Visitors to the area may also want to visit the Elgin County Railway Museum in nearby St. Thomas. The mileage works in reverse as London, ON was formerly mile **0**.

Route Highlights

Port Stanley to Parkside
Lake Erie Spur

About to cross the Yarmouth trestle.

Miles 23–16: The King Edward lift bridge can be seen to the east at mile **23** while departing from the Port Stanley Station. As the train passes through the railway's yard, you can see the *Toronto, Hamilton & Buffalo Railway* caboose No. 71 near the shore of Kettle Creek, where it is used as a summer residence. As you cross Kettle Creek, look to the east look to see the HMCS Prevost Naval Reserve. At mile **21.5**, the Yarmouth Trestle offers good views to both sides, and they continue as the train passes by local orchards. Union Station, possibly the smallest union station in Canada, is passed at mile **20.6**; this flag stop station was built in the 1920s to serve a couple of local villages. Whytes, at mile **19.5**, features a CN snowplow, caboose, and other rail equipment for visitors to view. Seen to the east, the St. Thomas Psychiatric Hospital at mile **18** was not opened until after its Second World War incarnation as a Royal Air Force Training Centre. Passing the backyards of homes in St. Thomas, the train reaches mile **16.4**, where you see Parkside High School to the east.

York-Durham Heritage

Located about an hour northeast of Toronto, ON, the *York-Durham Heritage Railway* runs between Uxbridge and Stouffville. Connecting the two communities, the train travels through the Oak Ridges Moraine. It is operated June through October, on weekends and holiday Mondays. For more information, contact York-Durham Heritage Railway, PO Box 462, Stouffville, ON L4A 7Z7. Call: 905-852-3696. Web: *www.ydhr.on.ca*

Route Highlights

Uxbridge to Stouffville
York-Durham Railway

Miles 28–40: Your journey begins at Uxbridge station, built in 1904 for the *Toronto and Nipissing Railway.* The station has a unique design known as a Witch's Hat. On your way out of Uxbridge, you see the H.H. Goode and Son Limited seed plant to the east as the train travels past residential back yards. Lookout Curve, at mile **31**, is a great place to photograph your train. A large ornate farmhouse, typical of this area, can be seen on the east side of the tracks at mile **32**. Big Garibaldi Hill, the highest point in Durham Region, can be seen to the east at mile **34**. Also in this area the train passes a large pit to the west. Local pioneer Michael Chapman named his community's first tavern after his home in England — Goodwood House — which in turn provided the town at mile **35** its name: Goodwood. The forests, rolling hills, and farms of the area can be seen on both sides between miles **36** and **37**. At mile **38** the train passes Toronto's Granite Club golf course. At mile **39** the Stouffville water tower comes into view. You might see *GO Transit's* green and white bi-level passenger cars — which provide weekday commuter service to Toronto and return — just before arriving at Stouffville's modern station at mile **40.6**. Built in 1997, the station also houses the Whitchurch-Stouffville Chamber of Commerce and the Latcham Art Gallery.

York-Durham excursion train as it travels through Oak Ridges Moraine.

York-Durham Heritage Railway — Contact information on
page 142

South Simcoe Railway

Northwest of Toronto in the community of Tottenham, ON, the *South Simcoe Railway* is reminiscent of branchline railway operations up to the 1960s. The most commonly used locomotive to pull the train is *Canadian Pacific Railway* No. 136, featured in the Canadian Broadcast Corporation's mini-series "The National Dream," which was based on Pierre Berton's novel. Located here is a large yard full of historic railway equipment, some of which is on display to the public. Travelling through the scenic Beeton Creek Valley, the trains operate from May to October. Contact the South Simcoe Railway, PO Box 186, Tottenham, ON L0G 1W0. Call: 905-936-5815. Web: *www.steamtrain.com*

Route Highlights

Tottenham to Beaton
South Simcoe Railway

Miles 54–59: Departing the South Simcoe yard at mile **54.9**, the train passes the railway's collection of historic rail equipment.

Miles **55–56**: Curving to the northeast, the train crosses a high fill offering great views to both sides. At mile **57**, the Beeton Creek can be seen to the east.

The *South Simcoe Railway* passes underneath the *Canadian Pacific* mainline. Watch for modern diesel locomotives and long freight trains on the CPR ... "Yesterday meets today." Then the Beeton Creek is crossed before reaching the station sign at Nowhere, mile **58.4**. Beeton and the end of the line is reached at mile **59**—the train then returns to Tottenham.

Former CPR steam locomotive 136, with train, is ready at Tottenham.

Prairie Dog Central

The *Prairie Dog Central* in Manitoba gives passengers a glimpse of what it was like to cross the prairies by rail at the turn of the century. The train is pulled by either a vintage 1952 diesel locomotive or by steam locomotive No. 3. The latter originally worked for the *Canadian Pacific Railway,* then subsequently for *Winnipeg Hydro* between Lac du Bonnet, Pointe du Bois, and Slave Falls for the *City Hydro Tramway.* Passengers travel in grand style in restored wooden coaches which feature fully-restored interiors. The train operates from mid-May to the end of September. For more information, contact the Vintage Locomotive Society, PO Box 33021, RPO Polo Park, Winnipeg, MB R3G 3N4. Call: 204-832-5259. Web: *www.vintagelocomotivesociety.mb.ca*

Route Highlights

Inkster Junction to Warren
Oak Point Subdivision

Miles 9–27.5: Departing from the Inkster Junction station (built in 1910 and once situated in St. James at mile **7.6**), the train passes the large building where the locomotive and train are stored and serviced. At Lilyfield (mile **11**), you see a large modern through-put grain elevator to the west. The rich soil of the Red River Valley makes for some of the best farming in Canada; between miles **13** and **16** the train passes fields of wheat, barley, and sometimes sunflowers. Grosse Isle is reached at mile **20**. The concrete foundation of a water tower and a simple class 1 station are located along the tracks. The land in the centre of the wye here (used to turn trains) is a Provincial Heritage Site—it is an example of natural prairie that has never been cultivated. At mile **21** a Hutterite Colony can be seen to the west, and to the east an old wooden boxcar lives on as a shed in a farmer's yard. You reach Warren at mile **26**. The train proceeds to another wye at mile **27.5** where the locomotive and combination coach will be turned for the trip home. While here, passengers can stretch their legs, see the locomotive up close, and visit the country market.

The *Prairie Dog Central.*   — *Murray Hammond photo*

Rocky Mountaineer

Before the last spike on the *Canadian Pacific Railway* could be put in place at Craigellachie, BC, there was a country to cross. The first Canadian prime minister, Sir John A. MacDonald, met with a group of prominent Montreal businessmen including the president of the Bank of Montreal, George Stephen; the Chief Commissioner of the Hudson Bay Company, Donald Smith; Richard B. Angus; and financier and railway promoter James J. Hill. These men, together with others, formed the Canadian Pacific Syndicate and began the steps to build a line across Canada to the Pacific Ocean. The new company quickly acquired the *Brockville and Ottawa Railway* in Ontario. Government financing built a line in Manitoba from Emerson, at the Canada-US border, north to Selkirk and east to Cross Lake. In British Columbia, the company employed experienced surveyor Major Albert Bowman Rogers to look for a southern route through the mountains for the proposed line. The demanding task of supervising and building the line across the Canadian landscape fell to William Cornelius Van Horne, who arrived in Winnipeg on New Year's Eve 1881, and began his duties as the General Manager of the *Canadian Pacific Railway* the following day. Under his guidance, construction teams worked east and west from Winnipeg, as well as west from Ontario and east from the Pacific, under the supervision of railway contractor Andrew Onderdonk. By 1883 the rail line had reached Calgary, but funds were soon used up because of the expensive construction in both the Rocky Mountains and the rugged Canadian Shield. The government told the company to expect no more funding, jeopardizing the future of the railway. Salvation came from an unexpected source in 1885, when the Metis people, led by charismatic leader Louis Riel, started the second Northwest Rebellion in Saskatchewan. Van Horne turned the railway's darkest hour into one of its finest moments by promising the government that the railway could move troops and supplies in five days to the troubled area to overcome the rebellion. Although troops still had to march through sections of northern Ontario where the rail line was not yet completed, they made it in five days and suppressed the rebellion. A grateful government pledged its renewed support for completion of the line. Thus, on November 7, 1885, with little fanfare and before a collection of railway employees, CPR President Donald Smith drove home the last spike on the railway. General Manger William Cornelius Van Horne proclaimed simply: "All I can say is that the work has been well done in every way." Soon after the line was opened through the mountains, tourists came to view the fantastic rugged scenery that challenged the railway. Today the scenery is best experienced from the Great Canadian Rail Tour Company's *Rocky Mountaineer*, which travels between Vancouver, Banff, and Calgary, as well as Vancouver to Jasper, on all-daylight two-day-long excursions. An overnight stop in Kamloops, where travellers stay in comfortable accommodations, is included in the ticket price. The trains run from April to October, with special trips in the winter months. For more information, contact at Rocky Mountaineer Rail Tours, 1150 Station Street, 1st Floor, Vancouver, BC V6A 2X7, Call: 800-665-7245. Web: *www.rockymountaineer.com*

Our journey begins in the city of Calgary. For overnight accommodation we recommend the classic railway hotel, The Fairmont Palliser. Call toll free: 866-504-4477. Visitors to the city will want to visit attractions such as the Eau Claire Market and the large Heritage Park, featuring heritage buildings from around Alberta, a working steam train, and an operating trolley car. For more information on these attractions and the world famous Calgary Stampede, we recommend you contact The Calgary Convention and Visitors Bureau located at Suite 200, 238 - 11th Avenue S.E., Calgary, Alberta T2G 0X8. Call: 800-661-1678. Web: *www.visitor.calgary.ab.ca*

Cheese and crackers served in the Gold Leaf dome.

Rocky Mountaineer — Contact information on page 146

Route Highlights

Calgary to Field
Laggan Subdivision

Miles 0–136: Calgary station is located in a modern mall near the Calgary Tower and the Fairmont Palliser Hotel. As the train departs the downtown area, you can see large glass and concrete skyscrapers to the north of the tracks. Then the Bow River comes into the view to the north, as the train moves through the Lawrey Gardens Natural Area. Between miles **5** and **6** watch to the south to see the high ski jumps built for the 1988 Olympic Winter Games. At miles **7.7** and **7.8** the twin bridges, each 65.8-metres (216-feet) in length enable the train to cross the Bow River (with help from a small island). To the south at mile **11** the train passes the Bearspaw Dam, built in 1954 to reduce flooding; the reservoir is also a source of Calgary's drinking water.

The earliest of Alberta's ranches were located near Cochrane (miles **22–23**). The train crosses the Bow River at mile **25** over a 125-metre (403-foot) long bridge. Ghost Reservoir, another source of Calgary's drinking water, can be seen to the north at mile **33**. Good views continue as the train travels past the foothills towards the mountains. The train crosses the Kananaskis River at mile **51.8**, before crossing the Bow River again at mile **53**. The entrance to the Rocky Mountains is at mile **55**; to the south are large limestone quarries from which Lafarge Canada produces over a million tonnes of cement every year. As you approach Canmore (mile **68**) watch to the south for the Three Sisters Mountain. At mile **72** the train passes the eastern border of Banff National Park.

Mount Rundle's steep cliffs are seen clearly to the south at mile **73**. Banff station is reached at mile **81.9**. This resort community, Canada's first National Park, is named after Banffshire, Scotland, the birthplace of two major financiers of the CPR. Formed around the hot springs on Sulpher Mountain, it was promoted as a tourist destination by CPR president W.C. Van Horne who said, "Since we can't export the scenery, we'll have to import the tourists." A landmark is the Banff Springs Hotel, which opened in 1888. Another east-west transportation route, the Trans-Canada Highway, can be seen above at mile **85**. Keep your camera aimed first to the south to photograph the Massive Mountain Range at mile **92**, then to the north for Castle Mountain at mile **99**. Morant's Curve (mile **113**) is a well-known photographer's spot. With the Bow River on the south side of the tracks and Mount Temple, Saddle Peak, Fairview Peak, and Mount St. Piran to the distance, this was a favourite venue of CPR's official photographer Nicholas Morant. The tracks divide between miles **116.2** and **123**. This separation, completed in 1981, reduced the grade for westbound trains to one percent and permitted significantly increased train speeds and freight capacity. At mile **116.2** the train passes the historic log station in Lake Louise, now a restaurant where you can dine inside the building or in former CPR dining car Delamere or business car Killarney.

Watch for the sign and small cairn at mile **122** (south side) that marks the Continental Divide. This is the highest point on the line and is the watershed where all water flowing to the east heads toward the Atlantic Ocean and to the west, the Pacific. It is also the boundary between the provinces of Alberta and British Columbia (as well as between Banff National Park in Alberta and Yoho National Park in BC). The train is now in the Kicking Horse Pass, named for the incident in which noted explorer James Hector was rendered unconscious for a few days when his horse lost its balance and kicked its rider while crossing the river. The source of the Kicking Horse River, the blue waters of Lake Wapta, can be seen on the north side of the tracks. This location was once known as Hector. It was the eastern side of what was known as the "Big Hill," so named because, when the railway was opened in 1886, the eight miles between here and Field featured a treacherous 4.5 percent grade. Imagine brakemen in the late 1800s, situated on the top of boxcars, controlling hand brakes as the train moved down the hill. This steep grade was reduced with the opening of the world-famous Spiral Tunnels, for which construction began in 1907. This reduced the grade to a more manageable 2.2 percent. Partridge, (mile **128**), is named for locomotive engineer Seth Partridge. At this spot, on August 9, 1925, after hearing a rumbling sound from the mountains above, he stopped his train and climbed down the mountainside to warn the occupants of the Yoho Station who escaped only moments before a landslide buried the area. The train remained on the tracks, having stopped a short distance from the path of the slide.

Keep watching to the north to see the Lower Spiral Tunnel and the Observation Point near the highway, before you enter Cathedral Mountain and Upper Spiral Tunnel at mile **128.8**. Here the train curves 250 degrees in the 992-metre (3,254-foot)

long tunnel, emerging 17 metres (55 feet) below the point where it entered. You pass the site of the former Yoho station at mile **129.8** before entering the Lower Spiral Tunnel and Mount Ogden at mile **131.1**. The train curves 226 degrees in the 890-metre (2920-foot) long tunnel, emerging 15.2 metres (50 feet) above where it entered before crossing the Kicking Horse River at mile **131.7**. A 54.5-metre (178-foot) long tunnel, built as part of the same Spiral Tunnels system, is passed at mile **133.1**. At mile **133.7** near the 150-metre (492-foot) long

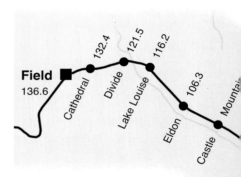

snowshed, the tracks rejoin the route built in 1884 and enter the 40-metre (131-foot) long Mount Stephen Tunnel, named for the CPR's first president, George Stephen. Arriving in the community of Field, the train curves around the former sectionforeman's house, close to the large black water tank, and stops at the flat-roofed station at mile **136.6**. The community was named for American financier Cyrus Field, following his visit to the area during the railway construction. Field is also the dividing point between the Mountain and Pacific Time Zones, so move your travel clocks and watches one hour back if travelling west or one hour forward if travelling east.

Route Highlights

Field to Revelstoke
Mountain Subdivision

Miles 0–125: In the days of steam, locomotives were added at Field to the trains for additional pulling power to help deal with the steep grades. The wide Kicking Horse River is clearly seen to the north; the route crosses the Kicking Horse a total of seven times, with one of these made at mile **9.2** on a 48-metre (157-foot) long bridge. Chancellor Peak Campground sits on an island in the middle of the Kicking Horse River and can be seen to the south at mile **14**. At mile **19** the train passes the western border of Yoho National Park. A mile later, it enters Kicking Horse Canyon. At mile **21.3**

lower one is the route of your train and the upper one is that of the Trans-Canada Highway, 150 metres (495 feet) above that of the valley floor (supported by steel stilts/beams). The train passes through Holt's Tunnel, named after a railway contractor, at mile **33**. At Golden (mile **35**), passengers once transferred from the train to sternwheelers that travelled south on the Columbia River, a practice that ended when the *Kootenay Central Railway* was completed in 1907. These tracks are now known as the Windemere Subdivsion; this is where the *Royal Canadian Pacific*, detailed on page 154, turns south.

West of Golden, the *Rocky Mountaineer* travels through the Columbia River Valley; good views are offered on both sides at mile **52.5** where the train

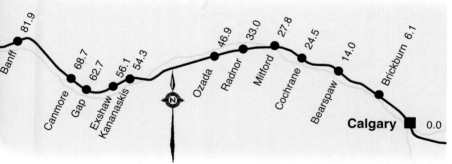

the train comes to the 94.4-metre (309-foot) long Palliser Tunnel. After you exit the tunnel, look to the river to see the starting point for white water rafting tours. The river is crossed again at mile **24.5** on a 71.9-metre (235-foot) long bridge. To the south, between miles **27** and **29**, there are great views of the river's rapids before you enter another tunnel at mile **30**. At mile **31** there are two crossings of the Kicking Horse River—the

crosses the Columbia River. The abandoned tunnel at mile **57** was part of a 1974 route change, when the headwaters of the Mica Dam flooded the original route between here and mile **66**. At mile **70** the train passes the eastern boundary of Glacier National Park, before crossing Mountain Creek at mile **70.8** and Surprise Creek at mile **74.4**. One of the most stunning views from any railway in Canada is at mile **76.2** — the Stoney Creek Bridge. Keep your camera ready for the view from the 147-metre (484-foot) long steel arch bridge across Stoney Creek, 99 metres (325 feet) below. Between miles **80** and **85** the train travels through Mount MacDonald by way of the Connaught Tunnel. Opened in 1916 by the Governor General of Canada, the Duke of Connaught, the tunnel originally featured two tracks. In 1959, the roadbed was lowered and single-tracked to make room for higher freight trains. Watch to the north at mile **85.5** to see the log station at Glacier, built by the CPR in 1916. Since heavy snowfall is common in winter months in the Selkirk Mountains, the train passes numerous snowsheds and avalanche detection zones. The train crosses the Illecillewaet River numerous times before the passing the west-

Route Highlights

Revelstoke to Kamloops
Shuswap Subdivision

Miles 0–128: Departing Revelstoke, watch to the north for the Revelstoke Railway Museum building housing CPR 5468, a Mikado class steam locomotive, business car No. 4, and a locomotive simulator. The third railway bridge over the Columbia River, at 341 metres (1122 feet) long, offers good views to both sides. Upon reaching the west side of the river, the train travels towards Eagle Pass, named after a story told about explorer

ern boundary of Glacier National Park at mile **95**. The Albert Canyon Lookout is passed at mile **102**. The Illecillewaet River is crossed again on a 68-metre (223-foot) long bridge at mile **122.3**. At mile **124**, the train approaches Revelstoke, named for Lord Revelstoke, who represented the English bank that loaned money to the CPR during a financial crisis when the line was being built. The train arrives at the modern station at mile **125.7**.

Walter Moberly, who reportedly fired a shot toward an eagle's nest and then, to find a suitable passage, followed the direction that the startled birds flew. Whether the story is true or not, the train enters the Eagle Pass at mile **9** through the three Clanwilliam tunnels, built in 1907.

Watch to the south between miles **12** and **14** for the green waters of Three Valley Lake; the red-roofed building is the 200-room Three Valley Gap Chateau and

Ghost Town. The track parallels and then crosses Eagle River at mile **18.5.** To the south, near mile **20**, you see the popular tourist attraction known as the Enchanted Forest. Also to the south, you can catch a glimpse of Kay Falls at mile **22**. The train crosses the Eagle River first at mile **24.4** on a 31-metre (101-foot) long bridge and again at mile **25.6** on a 32-metre

43.5. Then, at mile **44.1**, the train crosses the 177-metre (580-foot) long Sicamous Narrows Bridge; the bridge can swing to allow boat traffic to pass from Mara Lake to the south and Shuswap Lake to the north. Also to the north, watch for Sicamous Beach Park and the arched pedestrian bridge above the mouth of the

Beavermouth
Redgrave
Rogers
Fraine
Stoney Creek
Bear Creek
MacDonald
Glacier
Ross Peak
Illecillewaet
Downie
Albert
Twin
Greely
Canyon
Butte
Revelstoke
Stanwilliam 8.2
119.9
125.7
109.5
105.8
101.6
98.1
89.9
85.5
84.9
79.3
77.7
68.3
66.2
62.0
57.3
Donald 51.2
Forde 45.7
Moberly 42.0
Field
0.0
Ottertail 8.2
35.0
Golden
Glenogle 28.1
Palliser 22.4
Leancholl 16.9

(105-foot) long bridge. Named after a Scottish clansmen rally cry, Craigellachie (mile **27.8**) was also the rally cry to complete the *Canadian Pacific Railway*. Here on November 7, 1885, at 9:22 am, in the company of executives and employees (and 17-year old Edward Mallandaine—the only non-railway employee or journalist present), Donald Smith drove home the last spike. In the park on the north side of the tracks is a cairn that was built in 1927 (with a 100th Anniversary 1985 addition at its base)to mark the spot wth CPR caboose 437336 and the Last Spike Gift Shoppe.

The train continues to play tag with the Eagle River, crossing it numerous times at miles **31.1, 32.6, 36.9, 40.2,** and

Eagle River. Sicamous (mile **45**) once was a significant rail-way stop—it featured the five-storey Sicamous station and hotel on the north side of the tracks, overlooking the lake. It provided convenient facilities where passengers could dine during the station stop. It served as a summer resort until 1956 and was torn down in 1964. The tracks that lead to the south were built by the *Shuswap & Okanagan Rail- way*; today they are operated by the *Okanagan Valley Railway*. You can see why Lake Shuswap is known as the houseboat capital of Canada as the train skirts the lake for the next 25 miles. Photo opportunities continue along the lakeside, but disappear briefly because of tunnels at miles **47** and **51**. The route then begins its large half-circle trip around the end of the lake before Salmon Arm comes into view at mile **60**. To the north, at mile **62**, is the

Salmon Arm Nature Bay, home to over 250 species of birds and the largest nesting grounds of the western grebe. The train passes the downtown area of Salmon Arm at mile **63**. After moving through a ranching area, at Tappen (mile **70.5**) the train begins its climb up Notch Hill, so named for the ridge that separates the Shuswap Lake region and the South Thompson Valley. Although it may not look like it, the considerable grade here is steep enough to have caused the CPR to create a second route for its westbound trains.

The large horseshoe curve between miles **76** and **78** is the only one of its type in Canada and offers nice views to the south; this new route was completed in 1979. At mile **85** the train is over 150 metres (492 feet) above Shuswap Lake; at mile **87** Little Shuswap Lake comes into view to the east. Look into the forest along the tracks for bears at Squilax (mile **87.6**) which was named after a First Nations word meaning "black bear." The train then skirts the shoreline of Little Shuswap Lake between miles **90** and **92** before reaching the community of Chase (mile **94.8**), named for American gold-seeker-turned-settler Whitfield Chase. As the lush landscape changes to an arid area of ranchland and rolling hills, the lakes empty into the South Saskatchewan River, seen to the north at mile **96**. Watch on both sides of the tracks for the unique pillar rock formations called Hoodoos. Near mile **114** is the site where "Gentleman Bandit" Bill Miner staged his second train robbery. The American stagecoach thief successfully staged BC's first train robbery in 1904 near Mission, BC, getting away with over $7,000. After living in Princeton for a few years he travelled to the Kamloops area to do some prospect-ing—or, at least that's what the locals were told. Along with accomplices Shorty Dunn and Louis Colquhoun, their real goal was to rob the CPR's westbound *Imperial Limited*. One night in March 1906, they boarded the engine at Ducks and ordered the crew to uncouple the first car and move ahead a couple of miles. Unfortunately for them, the car they took was the baggage car, not the express car. They escaped into the night with $15 and a bottle of liver pills, but were caught a few days later by the Royal Canadian Mounted Police.

At mile **127** the train enters the City of Kamloops. The unique scenery on both sides of the grassy and sandy cliffs continues into the urban setting. The train transfers to the *Canadian National* Okanagan Spur, arriving at the former CNR two-storey brick station (mile **128.5**). Here passengers on the *Rocky Mountaineer* will transfer to busses that will take them to their evening accommodation.

Route Highlights

Kamloops to Ashcroft Subdivision Okanagan Spur

If you are travelling on the *Rocky Mountaineer*, your train departs the former CNR downtown Kamloops station on the Okanagan Spur and crosses the South Thompson River. Look to the west when on the bridge to see the North Thompson River and South Thompson River. Once across, the train travels through the Kamloops First Nations Reserve before curving to the west and joining the CN Ashcroft Subdivision. The highlights of the journey continue on page 105 with the details of the route of the *Canadian*.

Alberta Prairie Steam

*F*ormed in **1990**, *Alberta Prairie Steam Tours* has worked hard to develop a major tourist attraction with economic benefits to the area of east central Alberta. The company offers a range of day trips aboard steam- and diesel-locomotive-powered vintage trains. As well, most include a full-course buffet-style meal at the destination.

Trips are scheduled weekends and select weekdays during the summer and selected weekends during the winter. For more information, contact Alberta Prairie Steam Tours Ltd, PO Box 1600, Stettler, AB T0C 2L0. Call: 403-742-2811. Web: *www.absteamtrain.com*

Route Highlights

Big Valley to Stettler
Stettler Subdivision

Miles 50–72: All excursions originate from and return to the Stettler Station at mile **50**. The only problem with some of these trips is that you are bound to get held up by a gang of masked ruffians on horseback, who force the train to stop and then proceed to rob the passengers. Rumour has it that the bandits are really good guys who donate the money they "steal" to charities, ala Robin Hood.

Along the route in Warden (mile **55**) you'll see railway yards and maintenance-of-way buildings. The train arrives at the historic *Canadian Northern* station in Big Valley at mile **72.1**. Visitors will have a chance to explore the community of Big Valley and the Roundhouse Interpretive Centre, which offers a self-guided tour of these once-busy railway shops. Also at Big Valley is the newly-established "Canadian Railway Hall of Fame," honouring people, communities, and technology that have made a significant contribution to the Canadian railway industry.

Arriving at Big Valley, Alberta.   *—Alberta Prairie Rail photo*

Royal Canadian Pacific

With use of luxurious business cars, the *Royal Canadian Pacific* recaptures the golden era of rail travel with its Calgary–Golden–Crowsnest–Lethbridge and back-to-Calgary excursion service. Limited departures occur in the spring through the fall months from the CPR pavilion in Downtown Calgary. For more information, contact Canadian Pacific Railway Pavilion, 133 9th Avenue SW, Calgary, AB T2P 2M3. Call: 403-508-1400, or toll free: 877-665-3044. Web: *www.cprtours.com*

From Calgary to Golden, the route is covered in the highlights of the *Rocky Mountaineer* beginning on page 147.

Route Highlights

Golden to Fort Steele
Windermere Subdivision

Miles 144–0: Turning south, the *Royal Canadian Pacific* travels on the line built by the *Kootenay Central Railway* and follows the Columbia River, which divides the Rocky Mountain range to the east and the Selkirk Mountain range to the west. Historic railway stations can be seen at Spillimacheen (mile **102**) and also at mile **68**. Here in Lake Windermere, a short distance from the tracks, the 1923 log station now houses a museum. The tracks then skirt Columbia Lake, which turns into the Kootenay River. When the CPR chose Cranbrook instead of Fort Steele (mile **0**) as a division point, the latter's fate was sealed, and it quickly turned into a ghost town. Its history continues as the Province of British Columbia reclaimed the town in 1961, and turned it into a heritage park.

Route Highlights

Fort Steele to Crowsnest
Cranbrook Subdivision

Miles 95–0: Travelling southeast, the train continues to follow the Kootenay River. After Elko, mile **54**, the train travels northeast, past the large station in Fernie (mile **34**) which survives as the Community and Art Centre. Then you travel east after Sparwood at mile **17**.

Route Highlights

Crowsnest to Lethbridge
Crowsnest Subdivision

Miles 101–0: Departing Crowsnest, the train crosses the British Colombia/Alberta border. At 4:10 am on April 29, 1903, the town of Frank (mile **86**) was buried when Turtle Mountain gave way and slid 700 metres (2,300 feet) down the mountain side. It left a 640 metre high, 915-metre wide, 152-metre thick (2,100 feet by 3,000 feet by 500 feet) pile of limestone, killing over 76 people.

Route Highlights

Lethbridge to Sheep River
Taber and Aldersyde Subdivisions

Miles 2–87: Departing Lethbridge on the Taber Subdivision at mile **110**, the *Royal Canadian Pacific* travels over the 1623-metre (5,327-foot) long Lethbridge Viaduct, 96 metres (315 feet) high above the valley and Oldman River below. Construction began in 1906 and was completed on June 22, 1909. The train then travels north on the Aldersyde Subdivision past rolling farms and ranchland. A CPR surveyor named the town at mile **5** Vulcan, after the Greek god of Mount Olympus, because it was the highest elevation on the CPR across the prairies. Today the town has built upon the Star Trek theme and features a replica starship and a unique "Tourism Trek Station." The subdivision ends at Sheep River (mile **87**), and connects to the Macleod Subdivision.

Route Highlights

Sheep River to Calgary
Macleod Subdivision

Miles 31–0: As you travel north, the Calgary skyline eventually comes into view. Don't look for the station at Midnapore (mile **8.8**) because it is now part of the display in Calgary's Heritage Park. The train continues to navigate the tracks through Calgary and eventually returns to the CPR Pavilion.

Dining car *Craigellachie* before guests arrive for dinner onboard the *Royal Canadian Pacific*.
— *Royal Canadian Pacific photo*

Kettle Valley Steam Rwy

A **great** deal of the area's history was influenced by the *Canadian Pacific Railway's* Kettle Valley Subdivision. Today, the heritage of this railway that served the southern portion of the British Columbia interior lives on in Summerland. Excursions are operated from May through September. More information is available by contacting the Kettle Valley Steam Railway, PO Box 1288, Summerland, BC V0H 1Z0. Call: 250-494-8422. Web: *www.kettlevalleyrailway.org*

Route Highlights

Prairie Valley to Canyon View
Princeton Subdivision

Miles 13–7.5: The train departs from the Prairie Valley station, featuring the Trout Creek Trading Co. and the Rail's End concession. Because water availability was always a great concern to the early farmers and ranchers in the semi-arid climate of the Okanagan, the Prairie Valley Reservoir, at mile **12.5**, was put into place by 1903. The large concrete flume follows the railway right-of-way, transporting water from Trout Creek to the reservoir. The Summerland Rodeo Grounds are just beyond the flume. The line runs along the north side of Conkle Mountain, skirting the southern perimeter of Prairie Valley. At mile **11.5,** those who have keen eyesight might be able to spot the roadbed and the Little Tunnel of the Kettle Valley Railway across the lake. The line goes through a number of rock cuts as it enters Prairie Valley. At mile **11** the train passes over Fyffe Road. At mile **10.5**, as the train travels a horseshoe curve at Little Conkle Mountain, the view stretches north to Garnett Valley, another picturesque pastoral valley with more pastures than orchards. The Summerland town centre can also be seen from here. The station known as West Summerland, built in 1916, was originally located at mile **9.7**, but was removed in 1964 when passenger service ceased on the KVR; all that remains from the original building is the concrete water tower base. At mile **8** you can see the Scherzinger Vineyards and Winery to the south. Keep your camera ready to photograph the Trout Creek Canyon to the north, where Trout Creek cuts a deep path on its way to Okanagan Lake. A siding was built here by the KVR Society to allow the locomotive to switch to the other end of the train and pull the coaches back up to Prairie Valley. At this point, the Shay steam locomotive also must fill up with water for the return trip Passengers may detrain here briefly and view the Trout Creek Bridge, built in 1913 to enable the Kettle Valley Railway to proceed on to Summerland.

Alberni Pacific Railway

Although most of the logging camps on Vancouver Island are long gone, their history lives on, and is best experienced during the summer months. Passengers on the *Alberni Pacific Railway* ride behind Baldwin 2-8-2T No. 7, which began its career on Vancouver Island in 1929. This small but resilient locomotive worked at four different logging companies before being retired in 1972. Once again in service, the route begins at Port Alberni's 3100 Kingsway Avenue, then takes you along the industrial waterfront to the McLean Mill national historic site. For more information, contact the Western Vancouver Island Industrial Heritage Society, Site 125, C14, Port Alberni, BC V9Y 7L5. Call: 250-723-1376. Web: *www.alberniheritage.com*

Visitors are also encouraged to visit the Alberni Valley Museum featuring displays of the history of the area, and a growing fleet of restored logging trucks. For more information they can be contacted at: Alberni Valley Museum, 4255 Wallace Street, Port Alberni, BC. Call: 250-723-2181.

Route Highlights

Port Alberni to Maclean Mill
Port Alberni Subdivision

Miles 38–33: The train departs from the Port Alberni Station at mile **38.8**. Built by the *Esquimalt and Nanaimo Railway* in 1912, the station is located at the entrance to the Alberni Harbour Quay. Moving along the Port Alberni industrial waterfront at a leisurely pace, at mile **37** the train crosses the first of two wooden trestles, 24 metres (80 feet) above the Kitsucksis Creek. The second, at mile **37.4**, crosses 12 metres (40 feet) above Roger creek. The train moves through the lush forested Beaver Creek area before arriving at the McLean Mill National Historic site. Located here are over 30 restored buildings and structures depicting a typical logging camp where mill employees lived and worked. Visitors can view the milling process with the 1926 steam sawmill as the centrepiece of activity.

Alberni Pacific locomotive No. 7
— *McLean National Historic Site photo*

Okanagan Valley Wine Train

*T*he *Okanagan Valley Wine Train* offers a trip through BC's Okanagan region, passing orchards, valleys, and lakes in this scenic wine-producing country. The train operates from June to September; you might want to make an advance reservation. For more information, contact the Okanagan Valley Wine Train, 9th Floor East Tower, 11830 Kingsway Avenue, Edmonton, AB.

Route Highlights

Kelowna to Vernon
Kalamalka Subdivision

Miles 118–85: The train departs Kelowna, BC from the quaint station located at 600 Recreation Avenue. To the south is the Elks Stadium, home of the Kelowna Grizzlies. As the train continues through an industrial and residential area, keep watching to the south for the former headquarters of Western Star Trucks. The various vehicles they built, such as long haul trucks, busses, and even army vehicles, were put through their paces on the nearby test track. The railway tracks curve to the north and, near mile **110**, the Shadow Ridge Golf Course and the Kelowna International Airport come into view to the east. Some of the fields the train passes through grow ginseng. Duck Lake can be seen on the west side of the tracks. The community of Winfield is passed at mile **105**, followed by Wood Lake. After passing a stand of Ponderosa pine, the train turns to the west and travels on a small picturesque stretch of land separating Wood Lake on the south and Kalamalka Lake on the north. You find more great views of this lake, with its turquoise-coloured water, as the train skirts the lake's western shore for the next few miles. You may also get a view of more than you expected when the train passes the lake's nude beach! The railway roadbed divides the Vernon Golf Course before arriving at the end of the line.

Kamloops Heritage Railway

*T*he **"Spirit of Kamloops"** utilizes restored *Canadian National* locomotive 2141 to take visitors from the downtown Kamloops, BC historic CNR station for a trip reminiscent of the days when steam served this British Columbia interior community. The trip begins with boarding the train's heritage or open-air coach. The star attraction, of course, is steam locomotive 2141. After departing the station, the train's route will travel across the South Thompson River on a trestle bridge with great views of the river on both sides, arriving at the edge of the Kamloops CN rail yard before heading back to the station. For more information contact: Station Ticket Office and Gift Store, 6 - 510 Lorne Street, (Station Plaza), Kamloops, BC V2C 1W3. Call: 250-374 - 2141. Web: *www.kamrail.com*

Index